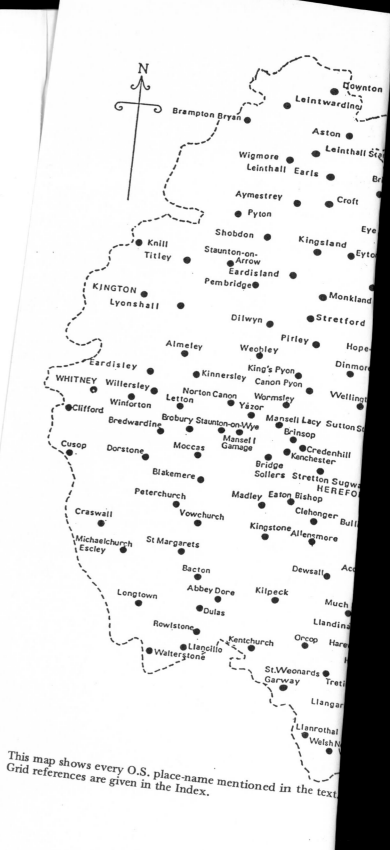

N

Downton
Leintwardine
Brampton Bryan
Aston
Leinthall Sta?
Wigmore
Leinthall Earls
Br
Aymestrey
Croft
Pyton
Eye
Shobdon
Kingsland
Knill
Staunton-on-
Eyto
Titley
Arrow
Eardisland
Pembridge
Monkland
KINGTON
Lyonshall
Stretford
Dilwyn
Pirley
Almeley
Weobley
Hope-
King's Pyon
Dinmore
Eardisley
Kinnersley
Canon Pyon
WHITNEY Willersley
Norton Canon
Wormsley
Wellingt
Letton
Winforton
Yazor
Clifford
Brobury Staunton-on-Wye
Mansell Lacy Sutton St
Bredwardine
Brinsop
Mansell
Cusop
Moccas
Gamage
Credenhill
Dorstone
Kenchester
Bridge
Blakemere
Sollers Stretton Sugwa
HEREFO
Peterchurch
Madley Eaton Bishop
Craswall
Vowchurch
Clehonger Bull
Kingstone Allensmore
Michaelchurch
St Margarets
Escley
Bacton
Dewsall
Acc
Abbey Dore Kilpeck
Longtown
Much
Dulas
Llandina
Rowlstone
Orcop Harev
Llancillo Kentchurch
Walterstone
St.Weonards
Treti
Garway
Llangar
Llanrothal
Welsh N

This map shows every O.S. place-name mentioned in the text.
Grid references are given in the Index.

THE DARWEN COUNTY HISTORY SERIES

A History of Herefordshire

JOHN and MARGARET WEST

Illustrated by David Bilbey

PHILLIMORE

1985

Published by
PHILLIMORE & CO.LTD.
Shopwyke Hall, Chichester, Sussex

ISBN 0 85033 570 1

This book is dedicated to
JOHN FOSTER SKEATH (1893-1958)

Printed in Great Britain at the
University Press, Oxford

Contents

List of Plates

List of Maps

Acknowledgements

The National Trust, for permission to reproduce plate 37; Anne Sandford BA, AMA, Assistant Curator, and the staff of the Hereford City Museum for all their help and advice, and permission to reproduce plates 14, 21, 31 and 32; Mr. R. Hill and the staff of the Reference Department of Hereford City Library, for much patient attention, and for permission to reproduce plates 1, 4 and 18; Miss Sue Hubbard MA, Assistant Head of Record Services and all the willing staff of the Hereford Branch of the Hereford and Worcester County Record Office for all their help and instruction; Mr. and Mrs. J.W. Tonkin for their encouragement and help; our good friend Joe Hillaby, for his wealth of knowledge and stimulating discussion; C.R. Elrington, General Editor of the *Victoria County Histories of England*, for his permission to reproduce drawing of artefacts from the Herefordshire volume of the *VCH*; Herr Axel von Welzrien for his kindness in showing us his castle at Mortemer; John D. Wallis BSc, MRTPI, Planning Officer, Malvern Hills District Council, for permission to reproduce drawings from *Ledbury Walkabout*; C.A. Campbell MRTPI, Chief Planning Officer of Leominster District Council, for information and photographs of Lion House, Leominster, and for permission to reproduce plate 34; H. Stephen Green, Assistant Keeper of Archaeology, National Museum of Wales, for reference to his notes on Arthur's Cave; M. La Biche, farmer of Sassey (dep. Eure), for showing us his redundant church; Mr. and Mrs. G.J. Williams for showing us the old school at Eye; Linda Ivell for all her help with photographic field-trips; Penelope E. Morgan FRHistS, FLA and Meryl Jancey MA, for their advice on records in the Cathedral Library; D.R. Wilson MA, Curator in Aerial Photography for the University of Cambridge Committee for Aerial Photography for advice on the Kilpeck air-photograph and for permission to reproduce plate 13; D.C. Allen, Librarian of Aerofilms Ltd., for his help in producing air-photographs of Croft Ambrey, and for permission to reproduce plate 3; The Director General of the Ordnance Survey; John Barrett, Assistant Editor of the Institution of Highways and Transportation, for considerable help on turnpike roads; J.C. Wilding, Diocesan Secretary for information about the diocese and its records; Elizabeth Evans, Agricultural Advisory Officer to ADAS, at Litley Court, for statistics and advice on Herefordshire's crops; Revd. W.I. McDonald, for help with the Woolhope parish registers; Mrs. Glenys Beech, Correspondence Secretary to the Offa's Dyke Association in Knighton, for information and newsletters about the Dyke and footpath; the County Council of Hereford and Worcester's Education Department, for up-to-date information on the county's schools; Lt. Col. T.J.B. Hill MBE for access to the Herefordshire Regiment's Museum; Capt. T. Marsh PSAO of C.Coy.5LI for his help on recent regimental history; Mr. and Mrs. Philip Lewis, for their kindly help and information about their house at Dinmore Manor; the many unnamed but helpful farmers who offered right-of-way and directions to hillfort sites; the incumbents of the parish churches who offered scholarly information on the fabrics and advice on village history; the Automobile Association for information on routes; David Bilbey, for his help with the maps and marginal pictures; John Roger, Chief Works Officer, City Surveyor's Department; Ron Shoesmith MIFA, Director of Excavations to Hereford City's Archaeology Committee; Prebendary C.W. Herbert, one-time Director of Education of the Diocese of Hereford, for his notes on 'The Background to the History of Education in the Diocese of Hereford'; the Hon. Mrs. Elizabeth Hervey-Bathurst of Estnor Castle, for kindly opening the castle out of season; the friendly staff at Tettenhall Library for their regular help with inter-library loans; J. Tullock, retired from the Highways Service, for his knowledge of the old roads; Angelo Hornak for permission to reproduce plates 10 and 27; Woodmansterne Ltd. and Hereford Cathedral for permission to reproduce plate 15.

Preface

Sir Robert Harley of Brampton Bryan, born an Elizabethan, was a stock holder in Virginia, and a notable parliamentarian. He was a leader of the Commons into Civil War, and his descendants became eminent Whig statesmen during the Glorious Revolution. Edward, his great-grandson, gave his name to the consultants' street in London. Harley once referred to Herefordshire as 'the most clownish county in England'. This unintentionally unkind reflection on a predominately rustic scene has too often prevailed, as an adverse opinion of the county's lack of influence on England's history.

Herefordshire, it is true, has few historic sites or great occasions to commemorate, at least in relatively modern times. There are no famous battlefields, no great palaces and few memorials. Apart from Harley himself, the county has produced no eminent national figures since the Mortimers of the Middle Ages. Herefordshire has no seaports to import new ideas or foreign plagues; there have been no invasion beaches nor bomb-sites. The county bred no martyrs, no rebels; there has been no class struggle. Industrial Revolution passed by; no teeming mill towns grew; there was no great depression. As George Eliot wrote, 'The happiest women, like the happiest nations, have no history ...' Lady Brilliana Harley, defending Brampton Castle against her husband's enemies, would have agreed!

Yet it must not be supposed that Herefordshire's remote situation on the border of the Welsh Marches had no historical significance. There were generations when a remote position, strategically placed to command the routes to Wales and Ireland, added a special importance to this English county west of the Severn. As a Celtic region of intensive settlement, a centre of the Roman frontier, the earldom of the last Saxon king, a Norman palatinate or an alliance of factious barons, Herefordshire sometimes re-orientated the direction of early English history. Here was a power base for Lancastrian usurpers and Yorkist king-makers alike. Later, during the Civil War, the King's dependence upon the county's resources and its communications with Wales and Ireland made Hereford a Royalist stronghold. In those days, English history came *from* the far shires, rather than taking place there.

Regardless of unwritten chronicles, the county is full of interesting places and unusual people. These make the pursuit of its real history a source of quiet enjoyment. Recent studies of Herefordshire's outstanding range of hill-forts recognise the county's archaeological importance. Other ruins, like the remains of Roman Kenchester, Abbey Dore or Wigmore castle, are worthy of more care and attention.

This is a county of man-made curiosities. Many of these, if not unique, are rare elsewhere. In Herefordshire, they are numerous. For example, nine parish churches have towers detached from nave and chancel, like Bosbury, Ledbury and Pembridge. The 44 castle sites mentioned by Camden are unusually thick on the ground. This English county's fount of Welsh place-names beyond the Wye at Llandinabo, Llangarren and Llanrothal remind us of Archenfield's earliest history. Offa's Dyke, too, is a massive reminder of the ancient division between Wales and Herefordshire.

Often we discover unexpected treasure. A pre-Raphaelite thatched church at Brockhampton, near Ross, mixes pseudo-medieval with Italianate and Byzantine styles. There is an unusual wall painting of Christ and the Tools at Michaelchurch Escley; Castle Frome's font was the centrepiece of a recent national exhibition. The rare wooden effigy of a medieval yeoman at Much Marcle would be exceptional in most counties (there are only 100 such effigies in England). Herefordshire has another example, that of a priest, at Clifford. The craftsmanship of Kilpeck's stone carvings is magnificent.

The county fostered many interesting people. From Stretton Grandison came Lady Katherine, whose claim to have lost a Garter challenges that of Joan, the Black Prince's bride. The womenfolk of Herefordshire certainly deserve more recognition by historians; Lady Brilliana Harley was more courageous than her husband.

The city of Hereford has a remarkable roll-call of theatrical personalities. These include Nell Gwyn, after whom Hereford's new theatre was named (in 1979) and the actor-managers David Garrick and Roger Kemble, namesake of an earlier theatre. Kemble's famous daughter was Mrs. Sarah Siddons, who acted with him in Hereford before making her debut as Portia at Drury Lane in 1775. The county has its share of poets too. John Masefield was born here, Elizabeth Barrett Browning lived here and Wordsworth wrote here.

There are still many valuable records of Herefordshire's past which are waiting to be read. In spite of the best efforts of the long-established Woolhope Naturalists' Field Club, with its invaluable range of up-to-date publications, there are many aspects of the county's past left unexplored. The beauty of Herefordshire's history is that you have to go to the county to learn it. This is what the authors, with great enjoyment, have endeavoured to do.

10

I Introduction to the County

The ancient county of Herefordshire was once the only whole shire, other than Monmouth, west of the Severn, with the most westerly English cathedral. Comparable in size with the counties of Cambridgeshire, Nottingham or Warwickshire, it was bounded to the north by Shropshire, to the east by Worcestershire and Gloucestershire, to the south by Monmouth and to the west by Brecon and Radnorshire. With Monmouth and parts of Cheshire, Shropshire and Gloucestershire, it was the centre of the English border counties, an English outpost on the Welsh border. It is now part of an uneasy amalgamation, named Hereford and Worcester, which straddles the Malverns and boasts of extending from the West Midlands and Warwickshire to Powys and Gwent, from the outskirts of Birmingham, to the Welsh border. We are concerned only with the more ancient shire.

Herefordshire coat of arms

'Herefordshire is almost circular, 31 miles from east to west, 108 in circumference ... containing one city and seven market towns. Being a land of frontier in all the wars between the English and the Welsh, it abounds with forts and castles, both of earth and stone, no less than 36 of the former and 8 of the latter appearing in Mr. Taylor's map of the county. Its air is so remarkably healthy that Serjeant Hoskins entertained King James I in his progress here with a morrice dance by ten old men and women whose ages together made above 1,000.' This description of Herefordshire is taken from a late (1772) edition of Camden's *Britannia*. The county's circular shape is also emphasised by a striking relief map in colour, which stands in the entrance to the City Library. This model shows the city of Hereford firmly planted in the very centre of the map. The city stands on a low central plain, with gentle undulating slopes and ridges rolling towards the Malverns in the east and stepping more steeply westward to the foothills of the Black Mountains and the Forest of Radnor.

Except for low ridges at Wormsley (700 ft.), Dinmore (500 ft.) and Sollers Hope (650 ft.), Hereford's central hills are of no great height. The dish-shaped central plain has a low profile, often as near as 100 feet to sea-level. The harder sandstone layers tend to round off as gentle, flat-topped knolls, rising no more than 400 feet above broad, low-lying river valleys. Eastward, the older pre-Cambrian rocks of Malvern top 1,000 feet. Westward, outside the county, Here-

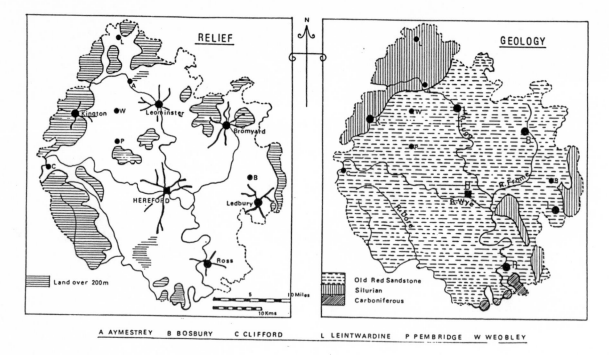

1. Herefordshire — physical features.

fordshire's red rocks lift towards the escarpments of the Black
Mountains, to the 3,000-foot summit of Brecon Beacons in Powys.
Along Herefordshire's western border, however, the foothills rise no
more than 1,300-1,700 feet from Kington to Cusop and down to
Longtown.

In the north, the Silurian 'edges' of Shropshire form a north-
western upland, rarely rising to 1,000 feet beyond Leintwardine.
Outcrops of older Silurian rocks at Woolhope and Aymestrey have
named their own limestone beds, which continue over the county's
north-western boundary. By Bromyard in the north-east, the Downs
rise steeply, their valleys draining into Frome and Leadon.
Southward, along the Monmow, Garway Hill climbs to 1,200 feet and
the land runs high towards Welsh Newton and Great Doward. On all
its boundaries, therefore, Herefordshire is ringed with higher ground
than at its centre.

High and low, almost the whole surface area of the county is
covered with Old Red Sandstone, some 400 million years in age. It is
this 'Devonian' stone which produces the county's characteristic
undulating ridges and a rich clay soil which breaks down to fertile red

loam. At its best, this is known as 'corn-stone', well suited to the cultivation of wheat-fields, hop-yards and orchards. Red sandstone was once quarried as building-stone fit for cathedral, abbey and parish church; the grey limestone provided building stone at Ledbury, Aymestrey and Woolhope. Nowadays, only the limestone is quarried, scarring the hills behind Leinthall Earls and dusting the lanes and hedgerows white. Carboniferous rocks, bearing some iron and lead, barely cross the south-eastern boundary near Ross and Whitchurch. Otherwise, Herefordshire has no worthwhile mineral deposits of coal and iron to exploit industrially. The blue-grey limestone of the south-east is more notable for its scenic features, the scarps and cliffs, the scars and caves, below which the Wye loops and meanders round Symonds Yat.

Central Herefordshire is a landscape of water-meadows rather than of mountain-sides. Five major rivers triangulate the county. Mainly, the Wye flows from the western border and meanders widely, southward into Monmouthshire. The Lugg, joined by the Arrow at Stoke Prior, flows north-to-south from Leominster. Two miles below Hereford, at Hampton Bishop, the Lugg passes closely by the city, joined by the Frome, coming down from Bromyard. Both rivers then flow together into the Wye in a broad confluence at Mordiford, near Fownhope. From there, the Wye wanders southward in great loops towards Welsh Bicknor, where the river becomes the southern boundary of the county.

Meanwhile, from the west, at Dorstone, the Dore follows its Golden Valley to join the Monmow, Archenfield's southern boundary from Walterstone to Welsh Newton. There it leaves Herefordshire to join the Wye at Monmouth as the river flows on to Chepstow and the Severn estuary. To the east of the county, Ledbury has its own river, the Leadon, which runs southward from Evesbatch through Ledbury and into Gloucestershire at Dymock, joining the Severn at Gloucester.

Herefordshire's basic physical features have always determined the patterns of man's habitation there, guiding his way of life throughout the ages, as inexorably as they shaped the landscape. Hill and valley, forest and river, stone and timber — all played their part in the county's history. These features stand today as ancient monuments, from cave and hill-fort to half-timbered street and sandstone church. Each village's field-shapes are the map of its settlement and progress; other maps, too, are marked by the lines of ancient trackways or straight Roman streets (still in use today), marching alongside abandoned railway lines and disused canal basins.

Long before the county's recorded history began, the sites of man's settlements were closely linked to passable trackways on the higher

Flint arrowhead (Vowchurch)

13

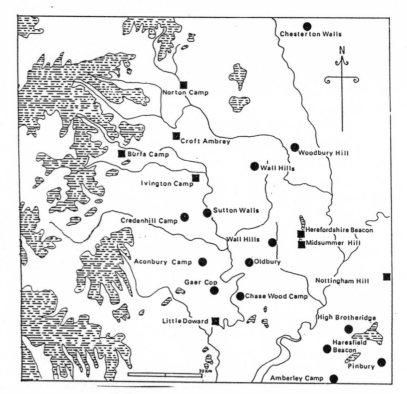

KEY: Over 15 ac. ● UNIVALLATE

■ MULTIVALLATE

▨ LAND OVER 300 m.

2. Settlement Map.

ground. Wandering prehistoric hunters kept to the ridgeways and the river terraces. The undrained lowland remained impenetrable to primitive nomads and stone-age farmers. By far the most ancient habitation in Herefordshire is 'King Arthur's Cave', just within the county, two and one half miles north-east of Monmouth, in the limestone escarpment by Great Doward. Immensely older than Arthur's legend, this twin-chambered cavern was occupied continually, if sporadically, from the Ice Age until the Romans came to Britain. Its first inhabitants, other than the cave-lions and hyenas which made their lairs there, were paleolithic (Old Stone Age) hunters of 10,000 to 130,000 years ago. They used fire, flint and bone, as the remains in Gloucester and Hereford Museum show.

In the cave, amongst the scattered bones of mammoth, woolly rhinoceros, hyena, reindeer, bison, lion and bear, were found the primitive stone implements of Herefordshire's earliest inhabitants. During 1927-8, and again in 1955, explorers from Bristol University Spelaeological Society unearthed 200 paleolithic implements in King Arthur's Cave, including flint gravers, scrapers, awls and saws. Some of these appear to have been made to fit into slotted handles or shafts.

This collection, together with the published records of finds destroyed in the Bristol blitz, has recently (1984) been re-examined

14

by Stephen Green, Assistant Keeper of Archaeology at the National Museum of Wales in Cardiff. His notes, for which we are indebted to him, refer to the oldest worked flints found lying under a stalagmite floor of the last inter-glacial age, *c.*125,000 years ago. He also identifies a fragment of a stone spear-point of a time generally dated *c.*35,000 B.C. 'These artefacts', Green notes, 'occur in the Low Countries and across the Northern European Plain. They belong to a time when the Neanderthal population of Europe was being replaced by fully modern man, *Homo sapiens sapiens*, spreading into Europe from the Middle East. It is tempting to suggest that the makers of the earliest Upper Paleolithic tools may actually have been Neanderthals.' Most of the other identifiable tools in the cave belong to a later paleolithic phase, from *c.*10,000 to 8,000 B.C. 'The gravers would have been used for working bone and antler. The scrapers and awls belong together and were probably used for preparing hides and perforating them prior to sewing them together for use as clothing or for skin shelters.' These finds reconstruct a dramatic picture of our primitive ancestors. They squatted at work around hearths at the mouth of the cave, for which they had contested possession with the lions, bears and hyenas.

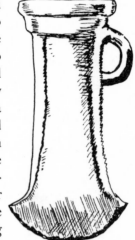

Bronze axehead (Vowchurch)

More recent by far, though still prehistoric, is the Department of the Environment site which overlooks the valley above Dorstone. This ancient monument is also attributed to the legendary Briton, as King Arthur's Stone. It consists of a broken 20-foot slab, or capstone, standing askew on several half-fallen upright stones. This was the stone lining of a communal burial chamber, the grave of tribal chieftains who lived 4,000 years ago, in the Neolithic, or New Stone Age. More advanced than their remote paleolithic ancestors, these people were farmers, who also used flint for their tools. Their huge grave was originally covered by a long earthen mound, or 'barrow', now displaced. It was 85 feet long from north to south, and concealed the surviving stone burial chamber which measures 18 feet by 17 feet and was approached by a curved underground passage-way. No burials were ever found on this site. Other grave-stones, or 'cromlechs', of this period have been found at Sutton St Nicholas, St Margarets and Whitchurch. Undisturbed, another neolithic long barrow stands above Eastnor, within an Iron Age hill-fort, near what the *VCH* refers to as 'traces of early dwellings'. The tumulus is a massive 150 feet in length.

The *VCH* describes how neolithic man 'made his tools of flint, stone and numerous other materials, grinding as well as chipping those of stone, in order to obtain an even, keen cutting edge. Some of these neolithic people's tools have been found in Herefordshire – a stone

15

hammer at Kington, arrow-heads at Oldcastle and Vowchurch. A scatter of flints near Ledbury, including scrapers, cores and chippings, seems to indicate a workshop site of local manufacture.

Arthur's Stone

Near the long burial-mound at Eastnor is a group of different barrows, round in shape. These are later still, dating from the Bronze Age, *c.*1550-1250 B.C. Five more, both round and rectangular, are found within the banks of an even later (*c.*100 B.C.) Iron Age hill-fort at Little Doward. There were other Bronze Age burials at St Weonards and Llangarren. Unlike neolithic interments, these round barrows usually contain a funerary pot of cremated bones, as at Brandon, near Leintwardine. In some cases, as at Llangarren, the round tumulus has gone and only the interior stone chamber or 'cyst' survives. This contained not ashes but a crouching skeleton. Most of these finds were bronze hatchets or 'celts' with narrow blades and handle-sockets. These were found on the Ewias upland, south of Dorstone, and in the Ross region to the south-east. In Hereford, sword and dagger-blades were discovered; these are kept in the City Museum.

Thus we see some archaeological evidence of the existence of the earliest inhabitants who lived and died within the county, but only fragmentary knowledge of their way of life. Their earliest artefacts and burials are found upon the higher ground, or along the upper reaches of the Lugg and the Wye. Indeed, most of the county's Stone- and Bronze-Age remains have been found south of the rivers Wye and Frome. With the new use of iron axes and plough-shares, however, from about 100 B.C. the Celtic Britons and the Saxon invaders who drove them into Wales were able to drain the swampy meadows and clear the dense undergrowth of the central plain. Here more permanent settlements were built along the lower water-courses and valleys.

The places which would become the county's main towns – Ledbury, Ross, Leominster, Kington, Bromyard and Hereford itself – all stand at vital cross-roads and bridging points, commanding the main routes and passes from England into Wales. Hereford is the hub of a wheel of 108 miles circumference. It stands at the very centre of a dozen roads which radiate to every point of the compass. Like satellites on the perimeter, each of the smaller towns commands its own road junctions. Herefordshire itself would become a strategic cross-roads of later history.

1. Flint artefacts found in King Arthur's Cave (SO 540158), amongst the bones of hyenas and cave-lions.

2. King Arthur's Stone (SO 311431) stands on a hill above Dorstone. The uprights and cap-stones, burial chamber of a neolithic tomb, were originally covered by a long earthen mound.

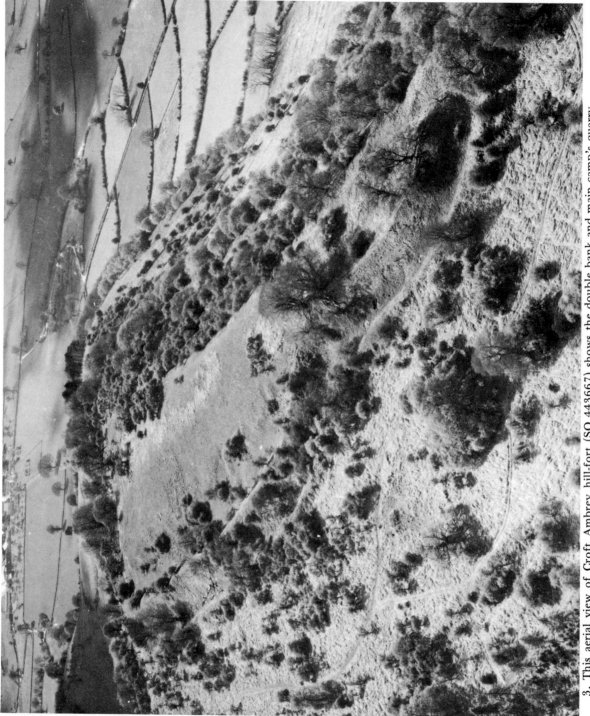

3. This aerial view of Croft Ambrey hill-fort (SO 443667) shows the double bank and main camp's quarry ditch on the south side, enclosing the plateau camp and house-sites. A hollow-way from the bottom right-hand corner leads into the East gate. Below the northern scarp, the minor road from Leinthall Earls swings round Yatton to join the later Roman road (A 4110).

4. Mosaic *in situ* at Roman *Magnis* (Kentchester). Similar tesselated floors of a villa were found at Bishopstone, nearby.

5. The Dyke passes under the A 438 at Bridge Sollers, to join a bend in the river Wye (SO 408428). The Offa's Dyke Path then follows the river southward until the earthwork re-emerges, briefly at Welsh Bicknor, finally at Ledbury on the Severn estuary.

6. Part of the 9th-century Saxon defences of Hereford, exposed at the corner of Mill Street, where a timber fence held back a rampart of clay and turf. Later, a stone wall was built in front of this palisade. This section is an archaeological reconstruction, open to the public.

7. The ruins of Mortemer Castle in Normandy are hidden behind a small chateau. A round tower stands on a motte, above the modern village.

II The Iron Age Hill-Forts

The most numerous, certainly the most conspicuous, monuments to Herefordshire's ancient past are the hill-forts which dominate the skyline and command the valleys. According to A.H.A. Hogg, in an important article, these rank high in British prehistoric studies: 'For any archaeologist concerned with the settlements of the pre-Roman age, Herefordshire is now one of the most important parts of Britain'.

Once attributed to a late Iron Age (c.600 B.C. to A.D.43), if not thought to be Roman 'walls', many hill-top sites are now dated as late Bronze Age, some as early as 1,000 B.C. This probably identifies the earliest builders as natives rather than a later wave of invaders from Europe. Modern techniques of dating, particularly the use of radio-carbon testing, a series of important excavation reports, revelations of air-photographs and consideration of previously unconsidered features, such as chambered gate-houses, post-holes and pottery-types, have all contributed to drastic re-interpretation of Herefordshire's Iron Age hill-forts. Even the term 'fort' must be reconsidered in the light of the excavations listed in this Chapter's bibliography.

The typical Marcher hill-fort is the irregular oval enclosure of a hilltop area of five to 50 acres, surrounded by an inner rampart standing 15 to 30 feet above an outer ditch, which was the quarry for soil and stone dumped to form a 'vallum' or bank. A single enclosure of this type is 'univallate', the ramparts tracing an ellipse around the contour of the hill about 100 feet below the summit. Large univallate enclosures – Aconbury, Credenhill and Sutton Walls are typical examples – are constructions of the late Bronze and early Iron Age. The strategy of defence was entrapment of attackers in the sheer-backed ditches below the rampart. Later the invention of sling-shots created new defensive tactics, giving a parabolic advantage, and longer range, to men behind a series of concentric ramparts – or their attackers. 'Multivallate' forts are found at Ivington, Little Doward and Midsummer Hill. A few sites, such as Aconbury, Ivington Camp, Sutton Walls, Wall Hills (Ledbury) and Coxhall Knoll, include more than one interior enclosure. One set of ramparts encloses an inner camp, another surrounds the outer annexe. These are probably the result of successive enlargements of the site, rather than a more complex initial plan or a separate cattle corral. Some inner enclosures

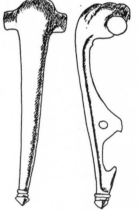

Brooch (Sutton Walls)

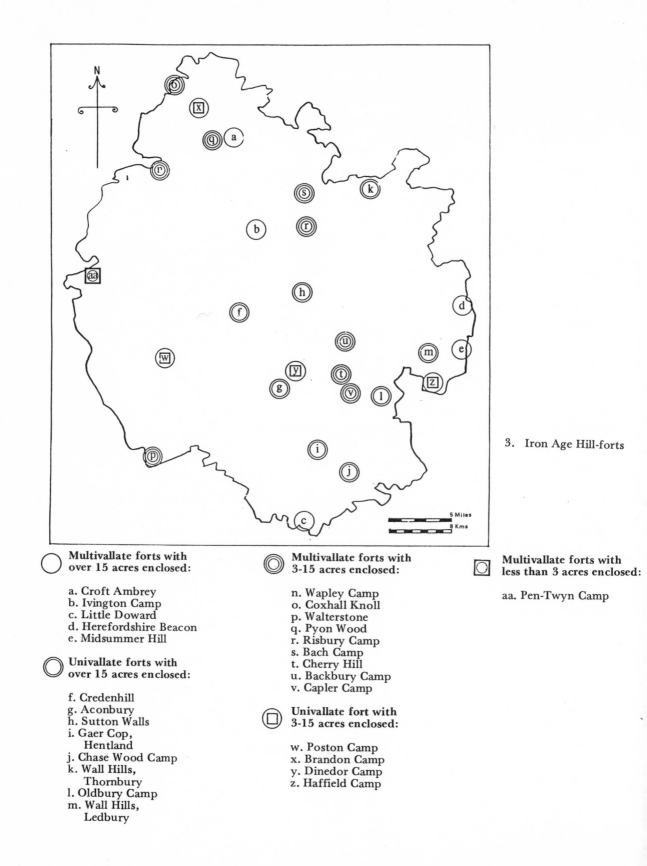

3. Iron Age Hill-forts

○ **Multivallate forts with over 15 acres enclosed:**

    a. Croft Ambrey
    b. Ivington Camp
    c. Little Doward
    d. Herefordshire Beacon
    e. Midsummer Hill

◎ **Univallate forts with over 15 acres enclosed:**

    f. Credenhill
    g. Aconbury
    h. Sutton Walls
    i. Gaer Cop, Hentland
    j. Chase Wood Camp
    k. Wall Hills, Thornbury
    l. Oldbury Camp
    m. Wall Hills, Ledbury

◎ **Multivallate forts with 3-15 acres enclosed:**

    n. Wapley Camp
    o. Coxhall Knoll
    p. Walterstone
    q. Pyon Wood
    r. Risbury Camp
    s. Bach Camp
    t. Cherry Hill
    u. Backbury Camp
    v. Capler Camp

▣ **Univallate fort with 3-15 acres enclosed:**

    w. Poston Camp
    x. Brandon Camp
    y. Dinedor Camp
    z. Haffield Camp

▣ **Multivallate forts with less than 3 acres enclosed:**

aa. Pen-Twyn Camp

may be of Roman or Dark Age date; on Herefordshire Beacon some work is Norman.

In some areas, ramparts faced with timber or stone revetments, or inter-laced with interior beams, may have displayed a conspicuous black-and-white pattern to the valley. In Herefordshire, a more ancient tradition of dumped ramparts continued, a technique which later came back into general use. Stone, timber and soil were the accessible building materials; occasionally blocks of workable stone were brought up from the valley. Entrances were built on a staggered, or passage-way plan, intended to isolate groups of attackers. It was once assumed that the defenders fought from the rampart-tops, backed by a palisade, but recent excavations have cast some doubt upon the whole idea of embattled farmers under siege. The inhabitants may have been defended by professional warriors who moved out of the enclosures to meet the enemy on the outer slopes.

Iron Sickle
(Sutton Walls)

There are more than 2,000 hill-forts in Britain. The forts of the Welsh border, from Shropshire through Herefordshire into Monmouth and Gloucestershire, are larger than those in Wales or south-west England, where there is an abundance of three-acre sites. The Marcher sites have more in common with a broad belt of larger forts, which spread across the Cotswolds and south-central England, towards Southampton. The Herefordshire group of sites is located around the future towns of Kenchester and Hereford; they are almost all univallate and larger than 15 acres. Some, like both Wall Hills sites and Sutton Walls, enclose 25-30 acres. Credenhill, most central, is largest of all, with 50 acres. The camp commands a clear five-mile radius before the next hill-site's neighbourhood is reached. Stanford extends this 'conjecturally controlled area' as far as Symonds Yat in the south, Brandon in the north and Herefordshire Beacon to the eastward. This area has a diameter of 50 miles, roughly co-extensive with the present county. The importance of communication routes, particularly along the river valleys, is evident. Other topographical features of slope, scarp and water-supply can be discerned on the ground.

By no means all the hill-forts tower at great heights – only Croft Ambrey and Herefordshire Beacon are more than 1,000 feet above sea-level. Some forts, like Croft Ambrey, are bracketed to a limestone scarp; others, like Poston, seal off a small promontory with earthworks. In most cases, one side of the site is protected by a steep natural slope, artificially enhanced by digging. Many forts stand above a gently sloping landscape, or a low-lying river terrace. These steep-sided flat-topped hills are mere knolls above a plain; their average overall rise is about 350 feet, usually above a brook, the broad valleys of the Lugg or the Wye, or the level course of the later Watling Street.

On the ground, one sees that each enclosure was sited for local command, rather than inter-communicating on a wider strategic plan. The sites fit the topography of each valley, or range of hills. Their defences face in different directions. Vulnerable gates are as likely to be protectively sited on the south or south-west of any camp as to the east or northward. The fall of the steepest slope may well, as at Aconbury, protect the east and south flank, or, as at Croft Ambrey, the north face. There was, as yet, no 'Welsh' or 'English' front.

Only the large multivallate forts – Croft Ambrey, Little Doward and the Beacon – rise as much as 600-700 feet above the surrounding landscape. Risbury stands only 60 feet above Humber Brook, Sutton Walls is a long, low ridge above the Lugg valley and Brandon Camp is a hummock, below the bridge at Leintwardine. These sites lend their aspect more to gentle slopes from which farmers would wend their nightly way uphill, rather than as inaccessible fortresses. The view from any of these hill-tops is always impressive, with a sense of commanding position. Ocasionally, the panorama is spectacular, with a sight of many counties and distant mountains. Yet, we should not think solely in terms of inter-communication or inter-connected outposts, but instead visualise permanent habitations, developed over a thousand years of continuous building.

The discovery that the enclosures at Croft Ambrey, Credenhill and Midsummer Hill were not occupied by a random scatter of circular huts as was the case in Dorset, Wiltshire and Caernarvon, but closely packed with regular lines of back-to-back houses of rectangular plan, has given rise to a new view of the functions of the hill-top sites. If indeed every one of those sites *was* completely residential and not, in some quarters, specialised to other uses as stores or workshops, the archaeologists' estimates of 75-100 persons to each acre of the enclosures yields impressive calculations of the population of Iron Age Herefordshire. Such an interpretation re-aligns the sites as economic bases of population rather than on a defensive frontier. Assuming a permanent settlement on every known hill-site, Hereford-shire's Iron Age population is now estimated as over 30,000. This is larger than Domesday's estimate (20,000) or later poll-tax returns (25,000). This population must have been more intensively organised than was once supposed of a sparse distribution of cattle-herders squatting in seasonal kraals of round mud huts.

If the hill-top sites are seen to be thickly and permanently settled, then each community must have been supported by subsistence arable farming of several thousand surrounding acres. So, the idea of

Skull
(Sutton Walls)

a pastoral people penning large herds with mound and ditch is also reversed. Small communities of a few extended families with slaves and dependents combined 500-strong to throw up the five-acre enclosures at Pyon Wood, Wapley Camp, Risbury and Cherry Hill. These, too, were domestic communities, rather than defensive outposts or signalling stations. Surprisingly, they are mostly multivallate, representing a disproportionate effort in man-hours of construction, compared with the looser single ramparts of Credenhill and Sutton Walls.

With 50 acres accommodating a possible population of 4,000 to 5,000 people, Credenhill would certainly merit the description of a 'tribal capital'. The most imaginative view of Herefordshire's Iron Age places this capital first in line of a succession of central nuclear settlements in the county, a line which continues with Roman Kenchester and medieval Hereford – the earliest of the county's townships.

Archaeologists admit a paucity of finds from Herefordshire's Iron Age sites. Away from the mass of the ramparts, their theories must be based on patterns of post-holes, fragments of pottery and a few carbonised wheat-ears. Metal objects are rare, Celtic coins more so. Staples and hinges for the gateways of the forts, the trappings of man and beast, are missing. In the hill-tops' acid soil, pottery dissolves, like leather and wood, so that these people were once thought to be aceramic. That would suggest a mobile, pastoral economy, at odds with a wheat-producing stability. The latter, with more pottery found in later excavations, is the more recent interpretation of the hill-top communities' economy.

For the layman, the variety of fragments in Leominster and Hereford Museums creates an intriguing picture of the 30 generations who rebuilt their houses as many as six times, each house standing up to 75 years before demolition. Over the same long period, they extended the ramparts, remodelled gates, manned chambered guard-houses and patrolled the vallum. They also lived and worked together. We can envisage a farming people inhabiting the central area of the present county as vassals of the Dobunni tribe, whose capital town was at Cirencester. Little is known of their identity. Tacitus, the late-contemporary (A.D.55-115) historian, son-in-law of the Roman governor Agricola, is imprecise about the population of this area, mentioning Silures, Ordovices and Decangi in turn. A problematic inscription on a Roman milestone at Kenchester gives the initials RPCD, usually translated as *Res Publica Civitatis Dobunnorum* (The State of the Dobunni People).

Sword blade
(Croft Ambrey)

21

Dobunni territory lay across the Severn, south-east of the Wye. To the south lived the Silures based on Caerwent and Usk, with the Demetae in south-west Wales, their capital at Carmarthen. To the north, into Shropshire, were the Cornovii, with a town at Whitchurch. Ptolemy, the Egyptian mathematician and geographer (*fl.*A.D.140), compiled a *Geography* which covered the whole known world, with lists of the latitudes and longitudes of various places. He gave the Cornovii another settlement at Leintwardine. Further north, around Wroxeter and Chester, were the lands of the Ordovices. It is a strange omission that no other tribal capital is mentioned in near-contemporary sources, so that a vacuum exists in our knowledge of Iron Age settlements on the Wye and the Lugg. Some historians fill this space with an Ordivician presence, others with a Silurian federation. Some attribute the *C(ivitas) D.......* of the milestone's inscription either to the Decangi or the Dobunni.

Vaguely presented in literary sources, these Iron Age people re-appear vividly at Sutton Walls as a group of mingled skeletons – men and boys, massacred prisoners-of-war – exhumed from a mass war-grave in 1950. From these bones a doctor recreated the victims' physical appearance, as an Appendix to Kathleen Kenyon's excavation report. At 5 ft. 8 in., an average inch taller than modern Englishmen, some were over 6 ft. tall. They had long heads, prominent jaws and heavy features. Some were strong and vigorous in their fifties; their teeth, though worn, were rarely decayed. Though the prisoners were armed with iron-headed spears, long swords and daggers, other excavations prove that their neighbours were usually farmers who cut their wheat with expensive iron sickles and herded belled cattle, sheep and goats with dogs. They hunted the hare and used oxen and work-horses on their fields. We know nothing of their transport, as there are no ruts in their gateways, few traces of metal or antler harness. Numerous clay spindle whorls, loom-weights, shuttles and bone weaving-combs tell of their fabrics, fastened by iron brooches, but no fragments of cloth, leather or sheepskin survive, nor any buttons or needles.

Their houses were smaller than the round-houses of the lowlands, which measured 18 to 40 feet in diameter. Herefordshire's builders erected 25 houses to the acre; a modern borough's planning department expects 16 houses to the acre. Theirs were set 11 feet apart, on 15-foot-wide streets. Space within the enclosure was at a premium, constantly used and reused. Single-storeyed, their ridges, roofs and hipped gables were covered with thatch, held down by limestone weights. The houses were possibly built on wooden platforms, as few sill-beams or clay hearths are found on the ground.

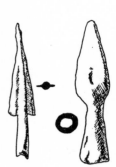

Spear head
(Sutton Walls)

Underfloor space was probably used for storage and headroom was sufficient to allow an upper sleeping-shelf, or storage space under the roof. Water was not usually available on the hill-tops, but was carried up from the spring-line about 300 yards below the vallum. The greatest hardship on the higher camps must surely have been exposure to intense winter cold.

Iron Age women baked wheaten buns in small portable ovens made from a very coarse pottery. Other pots were bartered, or bought from a Malvern production centre 30 miles from the Wye. This pottery was not ornate, but hand-thrown and simple in form, regularly stamped or incised with narrow rim-bands of chevron, wedge or cable patterns. At Sutton Walls, a curved design has been seen by the eye of faith as a 'row of ducks' motif, and a saucepan-pot takes its type name from Croft Ambrey.

The farmers were probably dependent upon craftsmen for all their metal goods. Slag and an anvil are evidence of iron-working at Sutton Walls, where an abandoned crucible contains a residue of molten copper. Metal was precious, whether for nails and rivets or as trinkets such as ornamental chain, pendants, rings and brooches. Bronze and flint implements were still in use. Ironically the seventh- and sixth-century people of the western marches' Iron Age are more accurately dated by finds of bronze weapons than by artefacts of iron. A hoard of bronze swords and barbed spearheads found at Broadward has given its place-name to a military tradition which extends from south-west Wales through Herefordshire and eastward to East Anglia.

Caesar differentiates between 'maritime Britain' south of the Thames estuary, and the 'interior' parts including the Marches. The later innovation of the Gallo-Belgic coinage in the south-east, firstly as a heavy currency of gold, suitable only for hoarding, or as tolls and tribute-money and, later, a more practical coinage of silver and bronze, did not penetrate much beyond the Midlands. Fewer coins earlier than those of the Roman occupation or an occasional stray, as at Leominster, are reported in Herefordshire. Nor are there any of the iron currency bars found elsewhere. Evidence of invasion of the hill-fort territory by immigrants is insubstantial. There was, apparently, no penetration of Belgic folk from the east.

Whether the later evidence of Halstatt and La Tène cultures, similar to those found in north-western France, was the result of immigration and trade rather than of sudden invasion, is another matter for conjecture. In any case, the picture is not simply that of a frontier or highland zone, with primitive tribesmen reluctantly absorbing foreign culture and assimilating alien invaders. Over so long a period of occupation of these sites, spontaneous cultural change was inevitable. Some hill-fort sites undergo one or more phases of refortification against – or by – newcomers. These changes are particularly evident during the third century B.C., but chronology is uncertain until the first century, with the Roman occupation.

Centuries of legend inevitably surround the hill-forts. Though none in Herefordshire is named *Caer Caradoc*, as are two camps in Shropshire and Clwyd, both Croft Ambrey and Ivington are supposed to have been defended by Caradoc or Caractacus, British king of the Catuvellauni around St Albans and chieftain of the native resistance against Roman occupation, before his final defeat by the legions 'somewhere in Wales'. Arthur, too, has his adherents, but most early observers saw the deserted sites not as royal palaces but as Roman 'walls' as at Sutton, Capler, Brandon and Cherry Hill. Though the hill-top sites were abandoned during the Roman occupation, it was likely that their massive defences and commanding positions would occasionally be re-used by attackers and defenders alike.

The 'palace' of King Offa of Mercia (757-96) at Sutton Walls was the legendary scene of the assassination of St Ethelbert, king of the East Angles, whose tomb gave Hereford Cathedral its famous martyr. (The story was re-told by the farmer at the foot of the hill in 1984.) The martyr-king is also associated with another camp at Dormington, which occasionally takes his name. Other sites are attributed to the Welsh prince, Owen Glendower (*c*.1359-1416), who was said to have defended Wapley Hill and Croft Ambrey against Lord Mortimer. As late as 1645, a Scottish Parliamentary army camped on Dinedor. In both legend and reality, the hill-forts are long-standing monuments to the Iron Age.

III Romano-British Herefordshire

A century after Julius Caesar's abortive reconnaissances in 55 and 54 B.C., the Emperor Claudius launched his conquest of Britain in A.D.43. Four legions and 50 auxiliary units commanded by Aulus Plautius, first Roman governor of Britain, invaded Kent, established a bridge-head on the Medway, and defeated the co-kings of the Catuvellauni, Caractacus and his brother Togodumnus, at Rochester. These were the sons of Shakespeare's Cymbeline, self-styled 'King of the Britons', their capitals at Colchester and St Albans. His brother slain, Caractacus fled westward into Wales. After Claudius's triumph at Colchester, the legions fanned out westward in pursuit and Plautius conducted a systematic four-year conquest of southern Britain. In the south, Celtic hill-forts fell like nine-pins to the weight of Roman armour.

By A.D.47, the frontier was marked by Fosse Way, from *Isca* (Exeter), through *Corinium* (Cirencester), *Ratae* (Leicester) and *Lindum* (Lincoln) to the Humber. In the absence of a deeper river-line than the upper reaches of Avon and Trent, the tenuous boundary was supported in its rear by a chain of Roman forts from *Dunum* (Hod Hill) in Dorset, to *Durobrivae* (Water Newton) in Cambridgeshire. An advance line was dug in to the west, parallel with the Fosse, southward from Broxtowe (Notts.) to Gloucester and the Severn estuary at Sea Mills. These forts, originally built in timber, became focal points for British civilian settlements or *vici* and, in some cases, later towns. By A.D.47, south-east Britain was a Roman province, the lead and silver mines of Mendip working for Rome.

The western marches remained unconquered. This threat, together with the incentives of lead, silver, copper and gold in Wales and the iron industry of Monmouth and Ross, drew the legions inexorably westward. Ostorius Scapula, Plautius' successor as governor (A.D.45-71), moved the frontier forward by campaigns against the Silures of South Wales and the Decangi in the north. In A.D.51, Caractacus was finally defeated on an unnamed battlefield which some have claimed, in the absence of substantial evidence, to have been in Herefordshire. Seeking sanctuary in Brigantian territory, Caractacus was surrendered to the Romans by Queen Cartimandua.

Britain was still susceptible to uprising, not only on the frontier, but also in the civil zone to the rear of the legions. The Silures took to a

Lion
(Kenchester)

25

protracted guerrilla campaign in the woods, bogs and hills. Under later governors, Britain settled down to moderate rule, culminating in the governorship of Agricola (A.D.78-84) who continued the advance into Wales. By about A.D.100, two stone-built fortresses marked the end of the frontier at *Deva* (Chester) and *Isca* (Caerleon).

As in the Iron Age, Herefordshire occupies a central, yet strangely unrecorded position on the Roman frontier. Watling Street marches northward from *Isca* via *Magnis* (Kenchester), *Bravonium* (Leint-wardine) and the Cornovian tribal city of *Viriconium* (Wroxeter), which was not fortified before A.D.60 but became the garrison town for two major legionary fortresses. This military zone was occupied by legionary and auxiliary forts, their camp-followers creating small Romano-British villages outside the walls. Leintwardine and Kenchester are examples of this type of settlement in Herefordshire. By the nature of its fertile river valleys, gentler slopes, well-marked routes and central position, the future county could be considered to have more in common with the lowland, civil settlement rather than the highland zone. Herefordshire's ambiguous position is blurred by lack of evidence, but aerial photographs now reveal more Romanization than has ever been excavated.

Some of the hill-fort sites, such as Poston and Sutton Walls, are covered with early Roman occupation levels. At Sutton, the grim discovery of the war-grave already described tells of Roman repression of resistance on those soon-to-be abandoned sites. At larger camps, a policy of evacuation and re-settlement of thousands of British settlers has been suggested. Many abandoned their isolated camps to settle near the Roman garrisons and share the benefits of their trade. At Credenhill, only a Roman temple now stood in the outer ditch. The earlier houses were demolished, apparently without burning or slaughter. Croft Ambrey and Midsummer Hill were destroyed by fire and there is an ominous charcoal layer under Kenchester's topsoil.

The three main settlements explored in any detail in Roman Herefordshire are the military depot and outlying camps at Leintwardine, the township at Kenchester, and iron-workings around *Ariconium*, now open fields near Ross. There are supposed villas at Bishopstone and Weston-under-Penyard, but these are as yet inadequately excavated. Kenchester is a focal point of the Roman advance westward and was possibly the site of a fort before the town walls were built in the second century. To the north, along Watling Street, *Bravonium* (Leintwardine) was an important military depot which reverses the usual Romano-British settlement pattern, as a native village which became contained within a fort. There were,

Cockerel
(Kenchester)

26

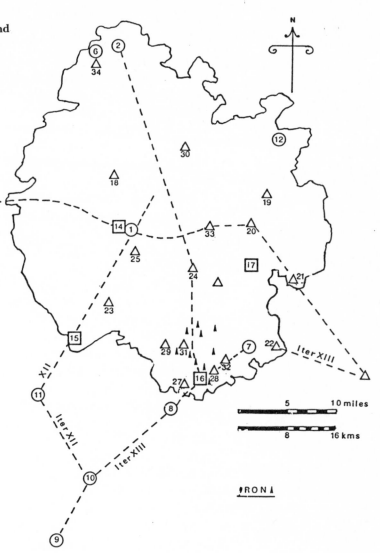

Romano-British towns and forts in and around the later county:

1. *Magnis* (Kenchester)
2. *Bravonium* (Leintwardine)
3. Jay Lane
4. Buckton
5. Walford
6. Brampton Bryan
7. *Ariconium* (Weston-under-Penyard)
8. *Blestium* (Monmouth)
9. *Isca (Augusta)* (Caerleon)
10. *Burrium* (Usk)
11. *Gobannium* (Abergavenny)
12. Tedstone Wafer
13. *Glevum* (Gloucester)

Mosaic pavements, possible villas:

14. Bishopstone
15. Walterstone
16. Whitchurch
17. Putley

Miscellaneous finds — (£ indicates coins):

18. Weobley
19. Bishop's Frome
20. Stretton Grandison
21. Donnington
22. Aston Ingham (£)
23. Abbey Dore
24. Dinedor (£)
25. Eaton Bishop
26. Fownhope (£)
27. Ganarew (£)
28. Goodrich (£)
29. St Weonards (£)
30. Stoke Prior (£)
31. Tretire
32. Walford (£)
33. Withington
34. Brampton Bryan

4.   Romano-British Herefordshire

successively, four forts within a few miles of the present village, at Jay Lane, Buckton, Walford and Brampton Bryan. When, in the second century, the military occupation was reduced, the region was overlooked by a quadrilateral of four forts, with a cornerstone at Leintwardine.

Except for the earthen ramparts at its north-west and north-east corners, little remains of *Bravonium* in the busy modern village of Leintwardine. Since the publication of the large-scale 1:2,500 Ordnance Survey sheet in 1903 (second edition), its traces have been even more concealed by new buildings, an overgrown churchyard and private gardens. The Roman fort's symmetrical 'playing-card' shape is unmistakable. Compared with Jay Lane and Buckton nearby, *Bravonium* was later (*c*.A.D.160-170), larger (4.5 hectares) and more permanent,and was a supply depot, housing a cohort of 500 men. The rampart, built of logs and clay, is ringed by successive ditches. The chancel of the church stands five steps above the nave, being built on one such *vallum*. High Street preserves the line of the main Roman north-south interior street. The medieval back-lane leads from Tipton's Lane outside the east wall and the site of the east gate is now concealed by buildings in front of the Methodist church. Church Street is diverted from the *via principalis* which connected the west and east gates of the fort. An outer annexe between the south wall and the river, in front of Leintwardine House, was the site of the soldiers' bath-house. Leintwardine was an important military station which maintained a persistent Roman influence in Herefordshire.

Magnis, now Kenchester, was not a particularly distinguished Roman town – it was too small to be a tribal capital. Its site now lies flattened under grass behind a farm yard. The farmer is irate at being denied planning permission to build a modern bungalow on the bare, flat site, and does not welcome visitors. The town's distinctive hexagonal shape, visible in the hedges around bare grassy fields, is clearly seen on ground and map, exactly bounded by the modern road to the south. The walls, now gone, enclosed a site of 22 acres, with east and west gates. The main street, reorientated at an early stage from north-south to east-west, is still marked by the field-path. Several foundations within the walls have been recorded, including public buildings with stone colonnades and a public bath-house in the north-west area of the town. A temple has been discovered at the roadside outside the east gate. The plan of *Magnis* was less orderly than that of *Viriconium*, a ribbon development along one main street. The streets were gravelled or cobbled, drained by stone culverts. Houses were timber-framed, with wooden verandahs, tessellated floors and hypocausts for central heating.

Bronze Statuette (Bishop's Frome)

28

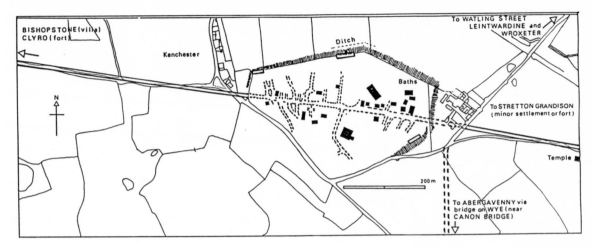

5. Kenchester

Interesting finds at Kenchester include an oculist's stamp and large quantities of well-worn coins marking a late period of Roman occupation. These indicate a long-lasting circulation of Roman money into the fifth century, after Saxon invasions had begun in the east. This is matched by a late phase of public re-building in the town. The livelihood of the townsfolk was dependent upon the entertainment of legionaries on leave from Wales or quartered nearby, and on the farm produce of local villas. A mosaic floor, found in the grounds of the rectory at Bishampton, suggests a drastic change in the life-style of some of the resettled Britons from the hill-forts.

In the south-west of the county, at Weston-under-Penyard and Bromsash, was the site of *Ariconium*, graphically described in the *VCH* as 'the Merthyr Tydfil of the Romans'. The scatter of Roman remains includes extensive areas of charcoal and slag which indicate the sites of furnaces and iron-forges. Widespread building debris, coins and pottery shards have also been recorded, but there is no sign of a well-planned town. The Roman place-name lent itself to the later Mercian kingdom of *Erging* and the medieval region of Archenfield.

A major source of information about Roman roads is the *Antonine Itinerary* (*c.*161-180), a road-book of 225 routes across the Roman empire. Two of these, Routes XII and XIII, link Roman sites in Herefordshire. The Roman mile – literally 'one thousand paces' – measured approximately one mile more to every ten English miles. In most cases, the modern distance exceeds the Roman distance of the *Itinerary*, due to the meanderings of later medieval lanes.

The benefits of Roman road-making in Herefordshire lasted 1500 years; the 'streets' were later used as coaching roads and motorways.

29

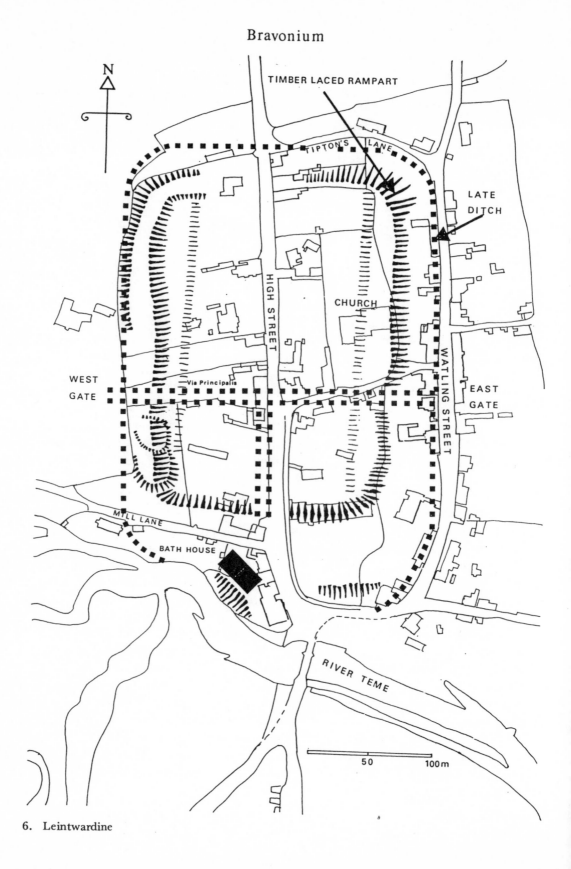

Bravonium

N

TIMBER LACED RAMPART

TIPTON'S LANE

LATE DITCH

HIGH STREET

CHURCH

WATLING STREET

WEST GATE

Via Principalis

EAST GATE

MILL LANE

BATH HOUSE

RIVER TEME

50   100m

6. Leintwardine

The main routes are clearly marked on the OS 1:50,000 sheets. For instance, the Roman road from Kenchester and Stretton Sugwas towards Stretton Grandison is the A4103; it loses the modern road between Withington and Newton, continuing across the fields through Yarkhill. At Stretton Grandison, a fort and minor settlement are recorded. Also well-defined is the Roman course of the B4215-A4172, from Stretton Grandison to Dymock and from Hereford to Leintwardine, now the A4110.

An effective method of locating lost sections of Roman road is to place a ruler across surviving stretches; in the intervals, straight fragments of minor roads, lanes and hedgerows will mark the course of the 'stony street'. Other Roman sections can be traced in this way between Stretton and Mortimer's Cross and from Mansell Gamage to Stretton Sugwas. Other 'inferred' roads have been explored, with reference to place-names, air-photographs and ancient maps, by enthusiastic members of the Woolhope Club, who have tested the concealed surfaces with soil augurs and confirmed the presence of the Roman surface. As *Stretton* – Sugwas, Bridge and Grandison – demonstrates, place-names along the routes record local traditions of Roman origins. Street Wood and Street Court indicate an otherwise lost section of Roman road south of Leintwardine.

Roman lamp (Stretton Grandison)

Other material remains of Roman Herefordshire are scanty. Some finds are displayed in the City Museum, particularly some fine mosaics from Kenchester, mounted on the staircase wall. Otherwise, apart from stray Roman fragments in medieval churches – a small altar at Tretire, a tombstone with a carved stone face at Upton Bishop – most other treasures, like the mosaics at Whitchurch, Walterstone and Weston-under-Penyard, and several hordes of coins, have been found, only to vanish again into private hands.

With the Romans' departure and Germanic settlement, the strategic east-west line of communication via Kenchester was no longer tenable and the town fell into ruins. The immigrants settled on a north-south line from Ludlow to Monmouth, passing through Leominster, with a new river-crossing at the 'army-ford' at Hereford. As tribal capitals and religious centres, Leominster and Hereford now superseded the more ancient sites. John Leland, the Tudor antiquary and map-maker, wrote in 1541 of an already grassy ruin, 'Kenchestre standeth a iii myle or more above Hereford ... this town is far more auncyent than Hereford and was celebrated in the Romans' tyme, as apereth by many things ... To be short, on the decaye of Kenchestre, Hereford rose and floryshed ...'.

IV The Mercian Kingdom

*Coin of
Offa*

The Dark Ages which settled upon Britain after the departure of the Romans were particularly obscure west of the Severn. In Herefordshire, unlike Worcestershire, there was no surviving Roman centre, no Saxon monastic chronicle, only a handful of royal land-charters. The county's place-names, which might tell the ethnic origins of Anglian settlers, have not yet been analysed. 'Herefordshire' in the fifth and sixth centuries did not exist.

The Romans withdrew from Britain in A.D.410. By 577 barbarian invaders from the south-west had isolated British resistance west of Deorham on the Severn estuary and on the Dee at Chester to the north in 613. Thus, Celtic Wales was effectively separated from England. It is important to note that the future county of Herefordshire lies westward, beyond this new Saxon frontier. It may be that earlier immigrants had moved into the region west of Gloucester by the river-routes and beyond the main area of settlement. Otherwise, the Romano-British inhabitants of *Magnis* and *Bravonium* perhaps sustained a twilight survival of a rustic Romano-British economy. Evidence of a late currency lends some credence to this idea. The Celtic Welsh preserved an unbroken link with Romano-British Christianity in Archenfield, as the Celtic cell at Kilpeck and a number of place-names and church dedications testify. Llandinabo and St Weonards are examples of this continuous Celtic Christian influence in Herefordshire. Dubricius, the first sixth-century Bishop of Llandaff, was active at Hentland and Moccas and there are dedications of churches to him at Whitchurch and St Devereux. Matched with this early Christianity, however, is the occasional suspicion of pagan associations in later Saxon churches – there are a number of 'Green men', witchcraft fertility figures, in the walls of Herefordshire churches, for example, in Leominster.

None of this is certain, however, until the seventh century – more than 200 years after the Roman occupation – when the land between Severn and Wye was occupied by an Anglian tribe, the *Hecani* or *Westerna*. Eastward, in the lands now Gloucestershire and Worcestershire, lived the Hwicce; it may be that the Hecani were the western Hwicce or Hwiccena. To the north of *Magnis* were the *Wreocensaetan*, populating the Severn's upper reaches towards the Wrekin. Politically, the region was part of the kingdom of the Middle Angles, whose

8. Weobley castle is long gone, but motte, bailey and gate-way are still well-defined under tall grassy mounds.

9. Kilpeck castle is not mentioned in Domesday and is more recent than the original Celtic church. Only the motte and fragments of a square stone keep survive.

10. The tympanum in Fownhope church was carved from local sandstone, c. 1140. It represents Virgin and Child, a winged lion and a bird. Re-erected inside the church, it once filled the head of a door-arch, as at Kilpeck. Its figures show the persistent influence of a sculptor of the Herefordshire school who had visited Santiago Compostella in Spain.

11. In Upper Sapey church, this Norman tower-arch, once over the chancel, has a typical zig-zag double moulding.

12. The south door of Kilpeck church is crowded with 12th-century carving. The pillars, twined with snakes, show on the left two Welsh warriors with ribbed leather jerkins, Phrygian caps and bell-bottomed trousers. The right-hand column develops a Tree of Life motif, repeated in the tympanum above the chevroned arch which supports two bands of grotesques. Above, birds and fish are linked by bearded masks; the lower band shows an angel, dragons a lion with a human face, an elephant and a phoenix.

13. An aerial photograph reveals medieval Kilpeck. The 12th-century church stands outside the castle's moat, between the motte and a pattern of village crofts enclosed by their own earthwork. A Benedictine priory stood to the south-east, beyond the photograph, to the left of the farm (*c*. 1600).

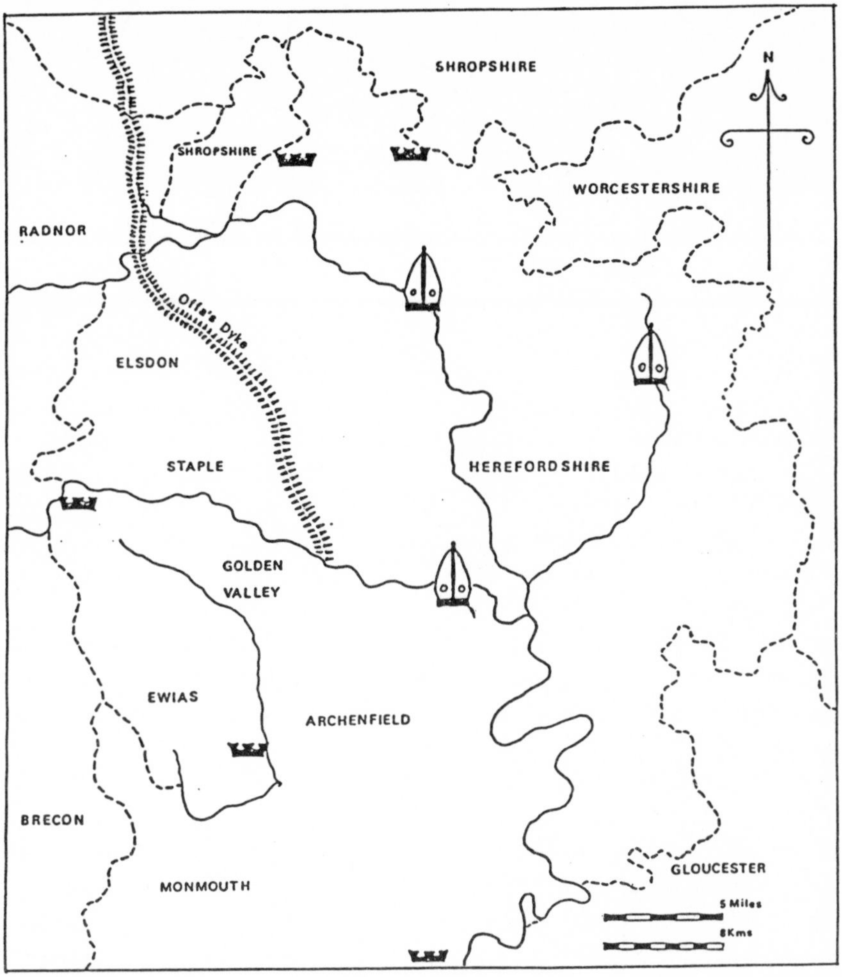
SHROPSHIRE
SHROPSHIRE
WORCESTERSHIRE
N
RADNOR
Offa's Dyke
ELSDON
STAPLE
HEREFORDSHIRE
GOLDEN
VALLEY
EWIAS
ARCHENFIELD
BRECON
MONMOUTH
GLOUCESTER
5 Miles
8Kms

7. Pre-Norman Herefordshire

conquests under the pagan Penda, king of Mercia (632-654), overcame the Christian kingdom of Northumbria. The western Hecani formed a sub-kingdom of Mercia, separately ruled for a time by Penda's third son, Merewalh (665-685), whilst his brother Aethelred succeeded to his father's kingdom and ruled Mercia peaceably from 675 to 704.

Penda's sons were converts to Christianity from two sources; firstly, from Northumbria, where the Irish mission at St Iona converted King Merewalh, through Eadfrith his wife, and secondly, through the Mercian kings' relationship by marriage with Kent, which looked towards Canterbury, the rule of St Augustine, and Rome. The rules and rites of the rival Celtic and Roman churches were different, but in 664, during Merewalh's reign, the Synod of Whitby ruled in favour of Roman supremacy, turning England's face once more towards Europe. Meanwhile, Merewalh founded a minster for Queen Eadfrith at Leominster, the religious centre of his western kingdom. The mother diocese of the Mercians was ruled from Lichfield at a time when there were only three sees in England, and Lichfield might lay claim to being a third archbishopric.

Merewalh's sons by his first marriage, Merchelm and Mildfrith, succeeded him as sub-kings of the Hecani. His second wife, Eormenberg, was a princess of the house of King Ethelbert of Kent, patron of St Augustine. Under Mildfrith, the religious centre of influence of the tribal kingdom was moved southward from Leominster to Hereford, where another minster church was built. Under the wider influence of Mildfrith's uncle, King Aethelred of Mercia, a more fundamental religious re-orientation took place. Archbishop Theodore of Tarsus, representing Rome, had divided the English provinces into 14 tribal dioceses. As a result, at some time after 676 the great diocese of Lichfield was broken into separate *parochiae* for each tribe. There were to be separate sees for the Hecani and Hwicce based on surviving Roman *castra*. Lichfield and Hereford were close approximations to *Letocetum* and *Magnis*.

Hereford was still, however, a *tribal* diocese, where a prevalent Celtic tradition held firmly to the ancient idea of a pastoral bishop moving amongst his flock, rather than remaining seated on a fixed *cathedra* or throne at the centre. There was as yet no bishop 'of Hereford'. Indeed, there is some doubt as to who the first nominee was, whether Putta, from 676, or Tyrhthelm, who is traditionally listed as second Bishop of Hereford from 688. Nor was there yet any county of Hereford; folk and diocese were the original communities.

When Merchelm and Mildfrith died, *c.*704-709, the autonomy of the Hecani sub-kingdom came to an end. Mercia was then ruled overall by Aethelred, his son Coelred (709-716) and, greatest of all, his nephew Offa (757-796), who claimed the titles of 'King of the English' and 'King of the whole country of England'. Offa's monument, beyond his famous laws, was the Dyke which takes his name and which defined the western and south-western boundary of his late eighth-century kingdom. We find that Offa's *vallum*, dug from sea to sea between Wales and Mercia, abandoned more than one-third of the present county to the Welsh. In the north, into Powys, a few ancient English settlements, such as Burlingjobb, were excluded by the Mercian dyke and barely recovered by the Norman barons of Domesday. Offa's Dyke and several territorial documents such as the *Ordinance of the Dunsaete People*, the *Tribal Hidage* and some charters of the Mercian kings, acknowledge the separate identity of Archenfield, an area south of the Wye, predominantly Welsh in its laws, its place-names, people and customs. Later, the Saxon King Aethelstan

Saxon comb

34

(925-939), as 'King of all Britain', exacted tribute from the Welsh kings at Hereford, but still accepted the Wye as their boundary.

After Offa, the tribal name of Herefordshire's inhabitants was the *Magonsaetan* (*c*.811). At the same time, Wulfheard first referred to himself as Bishop 'of Hereford'. Only later in the ninth century was the shire based upon the town of Hereford. Edward the Elder (899-924), son of Alfred, reorganised the ancient Midland kingdom into defensive counties, each with a defended 'burh' as its administrative centre. Thus Herefordshire, as a county, lost the diocese's southern hundreds of Shropshire to Shrewsbury. The Hwicce to the east were divided among counties based on Gloucester, Worcester and Warwick. The county was smaller than the earlier diocese of Hereford, as it is today. Not until the reign of Canute (1017-1035) was the county referred to as Herefordshire. This was a relatively artificial unit, compared with the wider territory of the Hecani's original kingdom and their tribal diocese.

Offa's Dyke signpost

V Earl of Hereford – King of England

*Coin of
King Harold II*

A generation before Hastings, Norman control of Herefordshire assumed a peculiar significance in English history. The county and earldom of Hereford was both defended and contested by Saxon, Welsh and Norman rivals, and was a keystone of King Edward's pro-Norman policy. *The Anglo-Saxon Chronicle*, monastic records kept in several abbeys, including Worcester nearby, recount those struggles year by year. The Saxon *fyrd*, or militia, fighting bishops, Norman castellans, English and French earls, all defended Leominster, Hereford and Archenfield.

The premature plantation of Norman tenants and castles by Edward the Confessor, and the strange affinity of Hereford's soil and settlements with those of Normandy are an historical curiosity, still evident in the landscape of both the county and the Duchy. Before the Conquest, Herefordshire remained stubbornly English. Yet 'nationality' was, as yet, a curious innovation compared with the more ancient traditions of folk and family, earldom and tribal kingdom. For a short while before 1066, both old and new traditions were held together by Harold Godwinsson, Earl of Hereford, who made himself King Harold II of England.

England was united in 954, when the Scandinavian kingdom of York was suppressed by Alfred's heirs. The kings of Wessex ruled the earlier separatist group of Saxon, Mercian and Northumbrian kingdoms. The weak rule of Ethelred 'Evil-Counsel' (978-1016) encouraged renewed Viking conquests, and a Danish kingdom was established by Sweyn Forkbeard and his son Canute (1017-1035). Ethelred escaped to exile; his wife Emma later married Canute. Her son by Ethelred was Edward 'the Confessor'; her illegitimate great-nephew was Duke William of Normandy.

*Bayeux Tapestry:
Harold on horseback
(with hawk)*

Successor to an Anglo-Norse throne, Edward had spent nearly 25 years in Normandy. His reign was to be a turmoil of invasions from Wales and Ireland and rebellions within his realm. The focal point of much of this resistance was Herefordshire. The Saxon earls were capable of king-making or reducing the fragile concept of 'England' to local fragments. Godwin, wrote the chronicler, 'had risen to such great eminence as if he ruled the king and all England. His sons were earls and his daughter was the king's wedded wife ...'. Two of these sons, Sweyn and Harold, were successively Earls of Hereford, their

36

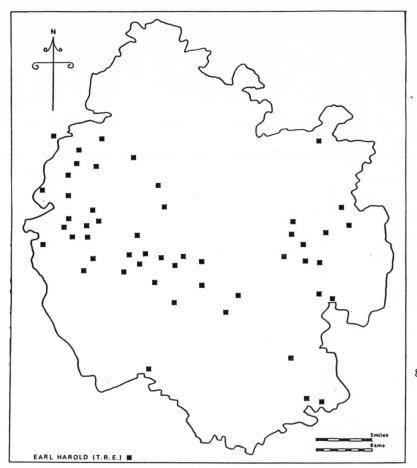

N

EARL HAROLD (T.R.E.) ■

5miles
8kms

8. Earl Harold's Lands

periods of office separated by banishment and the intrusion of a French nephew of the Confessor.

Hereford's border was beset by the continual struggles of rival Welsh princes, both named Gruffydd. One, son of Llewelyn, king of Gwynedd, conquered and ruled Wales; his rival Gruffydd was king of Deheubarth in South Wales. Each acted in turn as protector of English rebels and Viking invaders. In 1046, Earl Sweyn invaded south Wales in support of the 'northern Gruffydd'. In 1049, the 'southern Gruffydd' attacked Gwent, the Forest of Dean and the west bank of Severn. These Welsh incursions caused turbulent times for the county; the national aspirations of the Confessor and the Godwin family would have more far-reaching results.

In 1051, the Godwin earls rebelled and were driven out of England. Now King Edward could develop his Normanising policy to the full. This would directly affect Herefordshire's lands and people. First Robert, a monk of Jumièges, was made Archbishop of Canterbury and a Norman chaplain succeeded him as Bishop of London. Leofric of

37

Bayeux Tapestry:
Harold Crowned

Bayeux Tapestry:
Harold's Death

Mercia's son, Aelfgar, was given the outlawed Harold's earldom, but Herefordshire passed to the king's French kinsman, Ralf of Mantes, nicknamed 'The Timid'. It was this policy which built Osbern Pentecost's castle at Ewias Harold, and Richard Scrob's at Richards Castle. In 1052, the Godwins made a dramatic return with an invasion fleet and Harold succeeded to his father's earldom of Wessex. Earl Ralf kept Herefordshire, for the time being.

Now it was the turn of Harold's Mercian rival to be discredited. In 1055, Aelfgar was outlawed. He fled to Ireland and returned with ships and men to join King Gruffydd in Wales. 'Then,' wrote the monks, 'they raised great levies, and Earl Ralf gathered levies to oppose them at Hereford and they came together there. But, before a spear was thrown, the Englishmen fled, because they had been made to fight on horseback ...' – an interesting insight into a Norman failure to introduce feudal tactics to English thanes and housecarles.

Aelfgar's invasion was a disaster for Hereford. His army 'went to the town and burned it to the ground. The famous cathedral, which Bishop Athelstan had built, they plundered and despoiled of relics, vestments and all its treasures. They slew the inhabitants and others they carried off. Then levies were called out from all the neighbouring districts of England and they came to Gloucester and went a little way into Wales ...'; Earl Harold had an earthwork built about Hereford; when all the damage was done, the king revoked Aelfgar's exile and a peace-council was held by Harold at Billingsley, near Bolstone in Archenfield. Eventually peace was made and Gruffydd swore oaths to be a faithful under-king to Edward.

For the time being, political control lay with Harold. Leofric of Mercia died in 1057 and Edmund Ironside's heir, Edward Aetheling, a possible successor to the Confessor's childless reign, visited England, only to die in mysterious circumstances. Ralf, Earl of Hereford, died in the same year. The map shows how much of the county's lands had fallen into Harold's lands as the next Earl, and how tactically these manors controlled the roads westward into Wales. Earl Aelfgar was outlawed again, and again returned with Gryffydd's help. Harold continued to harry Wales from the north at Rhuddlan to Chepstow in the south. Harold's brother, Tostig, Earl of Northumbria, was banished and found a Norse army ready to support their own heir to Canute's English kingdom. In Normandy, Duke William awaited the fulfilment of promises which he claimed had been made to him by King Edward and Earl Harold. In 1065, the Confessor died and 'Earl Harold was hallowed king – and he had little peace in the time he ruled his kingdom ...'.

38

VI The Domesday Survey of Herefordshire

Domesday is England's oldest national record. Not all English counties were surveyed in 1086, but Herefordshire was recorded in significant detail. Entitled *Herefordshire, Archenfield and Wales*, the area surveyed was roughly co-extensive with the present county, though less well defined; the process of Norman colonisation begun by the Confessor was incomplete. Recently colonised lands beyond the Dore and Wye can be identified by their assessment in *carucates* or ploughlands, as at Garway on the Monmouth border. Anciently settled lands, some lying in Wales, were more traditionally assessed by the *hide* and grouped in military five-hide units such as Backbury, Wilmastone and Brinsop. At Brockhampton, the Commissioners distinguish between English and Welsh hides.

The western boundary lay along Offa's Dyke, down the Dore and Wye. To west and south-west, Archenfield and Ewias were sporadically recorded; here only 50 of the county's 300 Domesday settlements were recorded, many as 'waste'. At Longtown, Roger de Lacy pushed his defences to a new castle on the Monmow, barely four miles in advance of the earlier castlery at Ewias Harold. At Ralf de Tosny's castle of Clifford, Domesday emphasises, 'This castle is in the kingdom of England'. The record is also incomplete for the north-west upland and the western border. The central and eastern plain, in the valleys of the Lugg, Wye and Frome, were inhabited by eight to nine families to the square mile, with four to six plough teams. Along the western border, from Knill and Kington to Clifford, and in Archenfield to the south, there were fewer families (one to three) and fewer ploughs (one half to one and one half).

Archenfield is separately surveyed with its own laws and customs for Welshmen, who pay different rents in kind – honey, sheep, lambs and pigs. They were bound by English law in offences against English settlers, 'but if a Welshman has killed a Welshman, the relations of the dead man gather and despoil the killer and his relatives'. At Westwood, of six hides, 'one has Welsh customs, the others English'. The Welshmen of Archenfield also enjoyed the doubtful privilege of leading the army into Wales and bringing up the rearguard in retreat. The Welsh do not appear as a depressed subject race, but relatively prosperous, with some responsibilities, largely gathered around the castles. Some were mobile, only seasonally domiciled in a manor. At

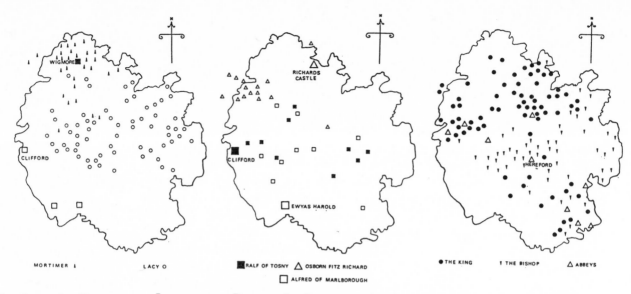

MORTIMER ¦   LACY O

■ RALF OF TOSNY   △ OSBORN FITZ RICHARD

□ ALFRED OF MARLBOROUGH

● THE KING   ┬ THE BISHOP   △ ABBEYS

9. Domesday Tenants

Longtown, Roger de Lacy received their rents and administered justice, 'whenever the Welsh are there'.

West of Knill and Kington, the territory of Mortimer, FitzRichard and the king drove a wedge into Radnorshire. These manors had been held by Harold's thanes and most were waste, as were other manors on the English side of the boundary, at Knill, Titley, Nash, Bradley and Middleton. Twelve places along the Lugg, including Leintwardine, Brampton Bryan and Adforton, were recorded in Shropshire's survey, as part of Mortimer's northern honour. In the south-east, confusion of the returns for Herefordshire, Gloucestershire and Worcestershire was the result of arbitrary arrangements made by FitzOsbern for payment of dues.

Herefordshire's tenants-in-chief make an impressive list of 38 prelates and barons. The king and Roger de Lacy held 75 manors each, and the Church of Hereford 58; these total half the county's Domesday manors. There were seven barons with 10 to 25 manors each; the most important were Tosny, Mortimer, FitzRichard and Alfred of Marlborough. Twenty-eight smaller tenancies had fewer than 10 manors each. The king's lands were in the north and south; apart from the castellan of Ewias, he is the only landlord south of the Wye. Lacy's lands spread across the centre of the county, along the Wye valley, shared by smaller tenants-in-chief who were his dependents. The church's lands were sheltered, lying along the fat, rich valleys of the Frome and Wye. The most compact honour was Mortimer's, linking Shropshire and Herefordshire around his castle of Wigmore and supported by the tenants of Richards Castle.

Many manors were stiffened by multiple occupancy or subinfeudation; most of the bishop's manors were held by men-at-arms.

40

Mortimer and Lacy held manors together at Bodenham, Wolferlow and Ledicote; Lacy as the largest tenant-in-chief is, inevitably, the most frequent partner, garrisoning Tosny's castle at Clifford, reinforcing the king's lands at Butterley, Eardisley and Stanford; alongside the bishop at Bishop's Frome, Collington, Tedstone Wafer and Wormsley. Some villages, like Ewias Harold, Marden, Munsley and Yarsop, accommodate the manors of as many as four major lords. The incentives of defence and access to main roads were matched in other places by the attraction of salubrious sites and the profits of mills, boroughs and markets. Nowhere does Domesday reveal these complex feudal tenures more clearly than in Herefordshire.

There is a striking resemblance between the countryside of Herefordshire and parts of Normandy. Particularly around Bayeux and Lassy, the dense *bocage*, orchards, timbered houses, hexagonal church-spires and wayside cider-mills are similar to those round Weobley, Wigmore and Whitney. The whole question of Norman origins and derivations is controversial. At Kilpeck, for instance, 'Anglo-Norman' style assimilates traditions which must combine Scandinavian-Frankish-Roman-Saxon-Celtic influences — or even those of pilgrims to the Romanesque cathedral of Santiago-de-Compostella in Spain. We cannot tell whether the Norman lord who paid for the work, a native master-mason, or imported craftsmen had their way with the style. 'Romanesque' in Herefordshire is not exclusively 'Norman'; we are more concerned with a Herefordshire school.

There is certainly less 12th-century Norman evidence in stone and earthwork, carving or castle-motte in Calvados and Eure than there is in Herefordshire. Little survives which is comparable with Leominster's massive naves, the font at Castle Frome, the tympanum at Fownhope or the chancel arch at Upper Sapey. This is perhaps an unfair comparison of a sheltered English county with the battlefields of France. Lassy is an outstanding example of the destructive effect of tank battles; French enthusiasm for the restoration of parish churches has been no less ruthless than Victorian zeal. In Eure's department, intensive farming eradicates much of the similarity with Hereford's bosky farms and orchards, but even there the 'dead-water' land around Mortemer's spire is seen from a little hill which might well overlook Ullingswick. Norman mottes are certainly not as thick on the ground around Pîtres, Ecouis and Mussegros as they are on the Herefordshire manors of their Norman overlords, Durand, William and Roger, at Weston-under-Penyard, Dilwyn or Laysters. At Mussegros and Tosny, ruined *tours* stand on flat ground. With the exception of larger castles, at Breteuil and Conches, most Norman sites bear out R.H.C. Davis's observation in *The Normans and their Myth*, that the motte and bailey was far from being general in pre-Conquest Normandy.

The most consistent similarities between Normandy and Hereford-shire are always those which involve trees and timber. The tall beech woods of the Forest of Lyons remind one of the Queen's Wood at Hope-under-Dinmore; a half-timbered farm-house in a back-street of Breteuil or an exceptional black-and-white street in Bernay might stand in Ledbury. Above all, timber porches, walls and roof-trusses in small unspoiled parish churches are, like Sassy, a redundant church, now M. La Biche's barn, similar to those found at Yatton, Gauciel and Aconbury. The open market hall at Lyons-la-Forêt is almost identical to Pembridge's, but the restored church at Epaignes cannot compare with the Norman font, tympanum and doorway at Alfred 'of Spain's' Domesday manor of Thornbury. It is evident that the Normans found more wealth in Herefordshire than they had enjoyed abroad.

Breteuil

Domesday is a second-generation document, compiled 20 years after Hastings, when many of the Conqueror's companions had been succeeded by their sons; one in five of Hereford's tenants is 'son of' an earlier baron. This was the case in the honours of Ralf de Lacy, Ralf of Tosny and Osbern, son of Richard Scrob; death and forfeiture had taken their toll. Domesday indirectly records two great political figures, dead in 1086, but still dominating the county's survey. These were King Harold and his successor as palatine Earl of Hereford, William FitzOsbern.

Harold II's abortive monarchy is ignored by William's commissioners. He remains Earl Harold throughout the survey, repeatedly accused of stealing the bishop's manors, as at Ledbury, Holme Lacy, Colwall, Coddington and Sugwas. Harold's manors marched across the centre of the shire, commanding the roads into Radnorshire. These manors were returned to the king and bishop, or distributed among 14 small tenants; Harold's thanes, Thorkell, Arkell, Aelmar and Britric, were replaced by sub-tenants with Norman names, like Thurstan, Odo, Godmund, Gilbert and Richard. Earl William's influence was longer-lasting. Lord of Breteuil, he gave the customs of that town to Hereford and many other English boroughs. He enfeoffed his dependents on the former lands of King Harold, set up castles and endowed his family foundations of Lyre and Cormeilles at Lug-wardine, Eardisland, Cleeve, Linton and Stanford. His tenants came from Tosny, Mortemer and Cormeilles, neighbouring fiefs in Normandy. Inter-related, they held land from each other in both Normandy and England. When FitzOsbern gave wasteland for the castle of Ewias to Walter de Lacy, it was no coincidence that the Lacy tenants were named William and Osbern. The Norman earl built castles on wasteland at Clifford and Wigmore and reinforced the pre-Conquest castle of Ewias Harold. In Hereford, FitzOsbern exchanged a piece of land with Bishop Walter, as a new market place, giving instead Harold's manor at Eaton Bishop. FitzOsbern's son, Roger, like many of his generation, was rebellious, supporting a 'foolish plot' of his brother-in-law, the Earl of Norfolk. He lost his inheritance in 1075 and the earldom of Hereford lapsed for another generation.

Herefordshire's Domesday manors are more difficult to identify as modern place-names than those of other counties. Darby and Terrett's *Domesday Geography of Midland England* points out that 'of the 309 Domesday places, 45% do not appear on the parish map of Herefordshire'. There are many duplicate names – Fromes, Hopes, Astons and so on – and 21 places are not named at all. Many have been traced by reference to ancient maps, to large-scale plans and later documents, particularly the up-dated 12th- century *Herefordshire Domesday*. These identify many Domesday manors as fields, woods and hamlets in larger parishes. *Capelfore*, for example, is now Foraway Farm in How Caple, *Colgre* is Cold Green in Bosbury. These identifications and many more are mapped in an appendix to Phillimore's *Domesday Book* of the county.

Other places announce their feudal allegiance more clearly in later documents, such as Kingstone and Kingsland, Bishopstone and Eaton Bishop, Holme Lacy, Stoke Lacy and Ewias Lacy. Brampton Abbotts gave grants to both St Peters and St Guthlacs in Herefordshire. Mansell Gamage was named later, from Gamaches, and the many Lacy villages were derived from Lassy in Calvados. Lyre Ocle, now Livers Ocle, in Ocle Pychard, was a gift to FitzOsbern's monastery at Lyre.

Herefordshire's Domesday villages present a rich social variety. Highest in the class structure were the Norman knights, each farming a small fee of about one hide with a full plough-team of eight oxen. Such men-at-arms are tenants of the bishop at Woolhope and Ullingswick. Indeed, a grant of land at Holme Lacy to Roger of Lacy for the service of two knights is the earliest record of a typical Norman enfeoffment.

Herefordshire's survey also records an unusual number of crafts and occupations, scarce elsewhere. We find manorial officials, reeves, beadles and foresters, with the lord of the manor's estate workers – millers, ox-men, cowherds, beekeepers and dairy-maids; there are 24 smiths and a carpenter. Some of these officials were servants of the king. At Marden, eight *servientes regis* are listed and another at Lugwardine.

Manorial customs are well recorded in Herefordshire's survey. Villeins did week-work for their lords at Linton, Marcle, Kingstone and Lugwardine; at Leominster, the villagers ploughed 140 acres of the lord's land and sowed it with their own seed. At Ross and Credenhill, services were commuted for cash, and at Alvington, now in Gloucestershire, the villagers paid an exceptional 20 ingots of iron. Other manorial duties are noted; in Archenfield, each villein's death-duty was an ox; at Kingstone, they carted venison as service. At Leominster, the charge for feeding a quota of pigs on fallen beech-mast and acorns in the lord's woods was a tenth of each man's pigs. There are a few free men, even in the half-conquered Welsh march; many more will have gone unrecorded, unless they rendered some manorial due.

A class of English riding-men, known as 'radknights', is widespread. Their duties were not military, but more in the nature of escorts and official carriers. They are numerous on the Welsh border and at Mansell Lacy, Yazor and Mathon. Twenty-five Frenchmen are mentioned, rich in plough-teams, settled as families rather than foreign communities. At Letton, seven men were settlers (*hospites*) with one plough and 5s. rent. Since the Conquest, much wasteland had been reclaimed, though some, at Harewood and 11 other western manors, had reverted to the chase. At Leominster, Weobley, Marcle and Fernhill, *assarting* (enclosure) had reclaimed the waste for farming.

The social structure of Domesday Herefordshire was marked by its frontier position and the waste of continual warfare. Unusual features of knight service, freemen, forest encroachment, French settlement and foreign customs, however, are not confined to a narrow boundary, but spread evenly over the county. Domesday is a rich source-book of early Herefordshire history.

Clifford Castle

VII Norman Mottes and Churches

The vigorous work of Norman builders and craftsmen is widespread in Herefordshire; much of this is outstanding in style and quality. A few fragments of pre-Conquest Saxon churches remain as vestiges of earlier walls, or foundations under later re-building; for example at Edvin, Hatfield and Bosbury. In the larger churches, such as Leominster, Bromyard, Wigmore, Fownhope and Ledbury, in the monastic church of Abbey Dore and in many parish churches all over the county, original Saxon and Norman buildings have been continually restored. There was regular work in lengthening the naves of older churches and re-roofing with heavy timber trusses during the more populous 13th and 14th centuries. Transepts, towers, aisles and chancels, with an occasional modern vestry, are the usual accretions to a surviving Norman nave.

The Duel
(Eardisley font)

Often, all that remains of an 11th-century church is a doorway, a window or two and a massive dog-tooth chancel arch. At SS Peter and Paul in Leominster, no traces of the original ninth-century convent survive, but the great 12th-century arcades remind us how massive Romanesque work could be. Equally remarkable as those large-scale survivals is the quantity of small complete parish churches of the early Norman period which have survived almost intact. Built on a simple rectangular plan, with continuous nave and chancel undivided by arch or screen, their thick walls are deepset with small windows, often the undecorated originals. Such churches are found at Moccas, and Castle Frome, amongst others. Even simpler, though heavily restored, are tiny Norman churches like Leinthall Starkes. Sadly, others are now abandoned ruins or redundant, as at Yatton.

These are complete or almost original Norman churches. Even more 12th-century work survives in substantial detail of doorheads, capitals of columns, chancel arches and fonts. In this ornate work, Herefordshire is rich indeed. Kilpeck is a nationally outstanding example of ornate and curious carving, reminiscent of the pilgrims' church of St James of Compostella in Spain. Decorations of the *tympanum*, the in-filling of the head of an arch or door-head, is an attractive feature of several Herefordshire churches. Tympana depicting Samson and the lion, George and the dragon, Virgin and Child or Lamb and flag are remarkable examples of Norman carving at Stretton Sugwas, Fownhope, Brinsop, Byton, and Aston.

Grotesque
(Kilpeck)

45

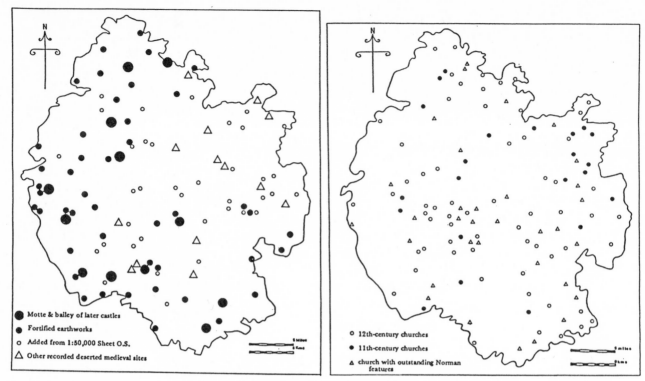

10. Norman Mottes and Churches

Legend (left map):
- ● Motte & bailey of later castles
- ● Fortified earthworks
- ○ Added from 1:50,000 Sheet O.S.
- △ Other recorded deserted medieval sites

Legend (right map):
- ○ 12th-century churches
- ● 11th-century churches
- △ church with outstanding Norman features

Figure on column of chancel arch (Kilpeck)

Plain and sturdy 12th-century fonts are commonplace in many Herefordshire churches, but the quantity of deeply carved, ornate examples is remarkable. These include fonts at Orleton, Castle Frome and Eardisley, thickly carved with evangelists, lions and the Harrowing of Hell. Intricately decorated too are the exceptional doorways as at Bromyard and Kilpeck. Chancel and tower arches with capitals rich in craftsmanship stand at Tarrington, Upper Sapey, Rowlstone, Garway and Kings Pyon; the doorway columns too are notable at Leominster, Yarkhill, Ledbury and Tarrington. At Kilpeck we see Welsh warriors dressed in fashionably pointed Phrygian caps of soft wool or leather, armed with long swords or, as at Eardisley, in quilted coats and conical helmets.

Scores of 12th-century sites are recorded on the distribution map. This shows clusters of early Norman churches surviving in the Mortimer honour to the north-west and in the solidarity of the bishops' churches around Hereford, Ledbury and Bromyard. This suggests an intensive 12th-century building programme across the Wye, into parts of Archenfield which had not been entirely English at the time of Domesday, nor even an integral part of the county or diocese. The map can only show *surviving* 11th- and 12th-century church architecture; its blank areas probably reveal places in which more extensive rebuilding of older churches was undertaken in the

46

Middle Ages. It is significant that sites marked on the south-west side of the map coincide to a marked extent with the contemporary phase of castle-building of the same period.

Herefordshire is thickly clustered with earthworks, many only small, half-hidden grassy sites. Built over two or three medieval centuries, these range in age and type from tiny rebel castles of the early baronial wars of Stephen's reign (1135-54), with temporary wooden towers and hastily dug mottes, to substantial castles of stone and, later, moated manor-houses well defended against border raiders. The first spate of fortification of these small manorial sites followed hard upon the Norman conquest. There is already a fortified house in the Domesday survey of Eardisley, a Lacy manor held by his sub-tenant Robert.

The Norman castle's pattern was that of motte and bailey, a round artificial mound thrown up by the excavation of a ditch and standing within a larger oval site which extended into an enclosed castle-yard, or bailey. At Wigmore, Kilpeck or Weobley, the walls were of stone, the baileys, or the street outside, packed with the burgage tenements of a small feudal borough. At places like Eardisley, the earliest enclosures and buildings would be of timber, vulnerable to rapid demolition. The spate of fortification which marked the troubled reigns of Stephen and Matilda was matched by a similar outcrop of new stone churches, themselves potential strongholds. The map shows the heavy weight of fortified medieval sites, especially in the west of the county. Those marked in black are the more substantial works inventoried by the Royal Commission on Historical Monuments. Some of these evidently housed busy communities.

Some charming details of medieval life, its work, sports, games and humour, are occasionally found in small remnants of masonry and woodwork in parish churches. The cathedral has a fine collection of these high-relief medieval wooden pictures. They include not only the familiar fables of fox and geese, grotesques and dwarfs, but also a few homely scenes, such as a domestic dispute where a husband has a plate thrown at his head! There is also a boar hunt, a stag at bay, a hawking scene and a horseback punishment which was actually recorded as taking place in the city as late as 1535. Most of these seats were made in the 14th and 15th centuries; there are other interesting examples at Holme Lacy, Madley, Leintwardine, Ledbury and Canon Pyon. In earthworks, masonry and pictures, the Middle Ages are brought to life in Herefordshire.

Detail of column (south doorway of Kilpeck)

Samson and the lion on the tympanum at Stretton Sugwas

VIII The House of Mortimer

No account of medieval Herefordshire would be complete without reference to the family history of the county's greatest barons, the lords of Mortimer. For a dozen generations, over a period of 400 years after Domesday, the Mortimers dominated the feudal history of Herefordshire and the Marches. They were, indeed, the epitome of Marcher lordship.

The term 'Marcher', from which 'Marquis' derives, strictly refers not to the border counties like Herefordshire but to those lordships which formed a buffer state *between* England and Wales. The extent of that territory came and went with Welsh re-conquest and, at its height, included large areas of Powys and Dinefawr which had been wrested from the Principality. The Marcher barons, Mortimers, Bohuns, Clares and Marshalls, had a vested interest in unrest. The king had given them all they could conquer, so that their lordship depended on continuing border warfare. Indeed, on occasion, they entered into separate agreements with the Welsh princes, to preserve their feudal power. If Wales were pacified, their rule had no further purpose.

In Edward IV's reign, the territory was placed under the jurisdiction of a new prerogative Court of Wales and the Marches. Herefordshire was included within this jurisdiction, but hotly contested its inclusion as an English border county, no part of Wales or its March. In fact, in earlier days, all Herefordshire beyond Offa's Dyke was Marcher territory. There, the Mortimers ruled, 'where the king's writ did not run', often directing the affairs of England from the honour of Wigmore. They made and unmade kings, married royalty, were guardians of princes or wards of the crown. On occasion, the Mortimers themselves aspired to the throne.

The family originated in Mortemer, near Rouen. Today, this is a quiet village, on the 'dead-water' of a low valley. Looking across to the spire of the church from the elevation of the ruined castle, one is inescapably reminded of many a Herefordshire village scene, as if one looked across the Lugg below Shobdon. Roger I was related to the Conqueror, but forfeited his castle because he gave shelter to the Duke's enemy, who was also Mortimer's feudal overlord. Although his son Ralf was the Duke's companion at Hastings, and was later rewarded by the forfeited lands of FitzOsbern's rebellious son,

Mortimer
Arms

48

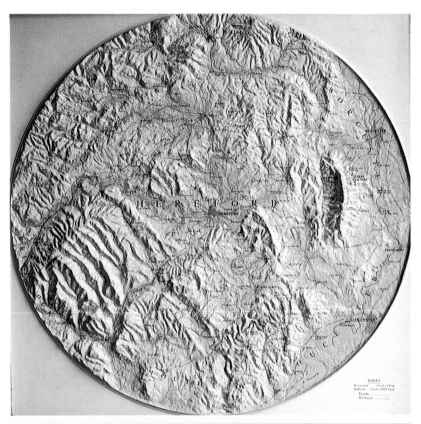

14. A relief map in the City Library's entrance emphasises the county's circular shape. Hereford is almost central on the plain, set away from the outer ring of hills.

15. These 16th-century effigies in Hereford Cathedral are the most colourful in the county. They commemorate Alexander Denton, in Tudor armour, and his wife in gown, ruff and girdle. Their dead child lies in swaddling bands.

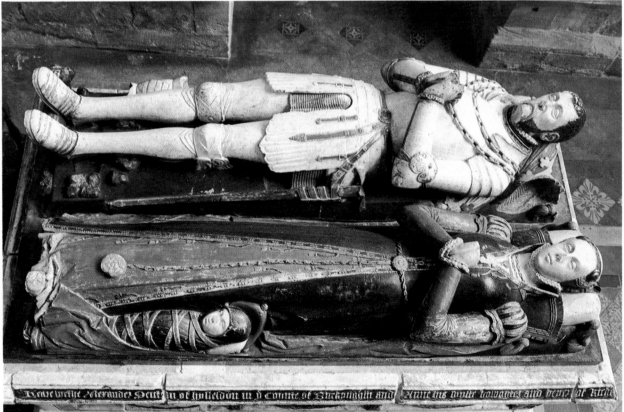

16. The ruins of the Mortimers' abbey are near Adforton, 1½ miles from Wigmore, now Grange Farm on the Roman road by Paytoe. The timbered gate-house is a late addition.

17. The Cistercian Abbey of Dore survives only in its lofty aisled presbytery and ambulatory. On the west side (left of picture) are remains of two columns and an arch of the ten-bay nave. Behind the church, to the north, are foundations of a cloister and chapter house.

18. Part of a monastic calendar from Hereford City Museum gives the saints' days for the month of June. The days of the month are reckoned by the Roman usage of counting towards the Nones or 5th, the Ides or 13th and Kalends or first of the (next) month.

19. A cider-press which stands outside the police headquarters on Bath Street in Hereford, like its fellow on Edgar Street, and the Museum of Cider in Grimmer Road, reminds us that there are still 6,000 acres of cider fruit orchards in the county, and that Hereford is a major cider-making city.

20. Kington is one of the oldest towns in the county, said to be named after Edward the Confessor. Its small market hall is still in use today.

including Wigmore castle, he never recovered his father's lost castle of Mortemer.

Ralf of Mortemer was Domesday tenant in 12 counties, his Marcher lordship based on Shropshire and Herefordshire. He also held land in Berkshire, where, like Cleobury in Shropshire, Stratfield Mortimer takes his family name. The Mortimers also held Domesday manors in Worcestershire, Warwickshire, Hampshire, Somerset, Leicestershire, Oxfordshire and Wiltshire. On the western Marches, their chief task was, inevitably, defence against the Welsh, conquering Radnor and Carmarthen for their Angevin kings. Five generations of Mortimers – Ralfs, Hughs and Rogers in turn – either rebelled against their English kings or fought their Welsh enemies. Hugh I captured Cardigan and built Carmarthen castle. Hugh II supported Henry III against Llewellyn, and his brother Ralf II built castles in Powys, at Cefn Llys near Llandridnod Wells and Knucklas, near Knighton. Their Herefordshire base was at Wigmore castle; their monastic foundation at Adforton nearby was their final resting-place.

*Wigmore
Castle*

During the Barons' war against Henry III, Roger III of Mortimer assisted Prince Edward in his escape from Hereford castle (on the city's legendary white horse) whilst Simon de Montfort was leading the baronial revolt against the prince's father. The king's party were based on Herefordshire and the Marches. Advancing against them, Montfort and the rebels were defeated at the 'murder' of Evesham by Prince Edward, supported by Mortimer. Roger III's son, Edmund I, continued to campaign in Wales, sending a Welsh prince's head to the king as a trophy.

During Edward II's reign, in 1315, Roger Mortimer of Wigmore and his uncle Roger of Chirk (near Oswestry) continued to hold the frontier. They joined Humphrey de Bohun, Earl of Hereford, the king's brother-in-law, to defeat a rising by Llewelyn Bren. Under Edward II's weaker rule, however, the Mortimers found themselves increasingly in opposition to the crown which they had made secure. Now the family led the baronial opposition to Edward II and his favourites, the Despensers. It was the Despensers' ambition to become Marcher lords which, in 1321, caused renewed civil war. Allied with the Earl of Lancaster, grandson of Henry III, the Mortimers rejected the authority of the Despensers. In 1321, the Earl of Hereford and the Mortimers captured London in defiance of Edward II's government, but Roger Mortimer was taken and sent to the Tower, whilst his confederates, like Clifford and Mowbray, were executed.

This was Roger IV, most notorious of the medieval Mortimers. Supplied by Adam of Orleton, Bishop of Hereford, with drink for the guards and a rope for the wall, Roger escaped from the Tower in 1323. He fled to France, having already formed his adulterous *mésalliance* with Edward II's queen, Isabella. In Paris, Mortimer lived openly with the queen, and was responsible for the custody of her 13-year old son, Prince Edward of Windsor. There, they plotted the invasion of England.

In 1327, invading Suffolk from Holland, Mortimer and Isabella advanced westward, pursuing Edward II into Wales. They occupied Hereford as their base, with the bishop of Hereford still in attendance as their agent. Orleton was sent to Monmouth, to fetch the Great Seal to Hereford, where writs were issued to summon a Parliament. In Hereford, too, they hanged Hugh Despenser. The king had been captured with Despenser at Neath. With Parliament's authority, Mortimer deposed him, in favour of his ward, the prince, as Edward III. At Berkeley Castle, kept by a man of the Mortimers, the deposed king was murdered.

Now Mortimer concentrated upon developing his power in Wales, as Justiciar or virtual suzerain. He was made, in 1328, the first Earl of March, a title never before bestowed on any subject. Claiming as he did succession from King Arthur, Mortimer saw himself as the king-apparent, acclaimed by Parliament at Nottingham with more enthusiasm than was accorded to the young King Edward III. 'He let the king stand in his presence', wrote the scandalised chronicler, 'and used to walk arrogantly beside the new king, never letting the king go before, but sometimes going in front himself.' It was the young Edward who struck first. He arrested Mortimer, an action which raised no rebellious response in Herefordshire or the Marches, took charge of government and summoned his own Parliament. Mortimer was sent once more to the Tower, still without support from Hereford. There he was charged with the murder of Edward II. Found guilty by common notoriety, he was hanged, drawn and quartered at Tyburn. His Marcher lands were given to William de Montacute, Edward III's supporter, as the first Earl of Salisbury.

Twenty-four years later, in 1354, Edward III restored Roger Mortimer V to his grandfather's earldom and estates, marrying him to Philippa, daughter of the Earl of Salisbury, and creating him, with the Black Prince, his son, one of the first knights of the new Order of the Garter. Roger's younger son, Edmund III, was married to the king's grand-daughter, another Philippa, daughter of Lionel Duke of Clarence. This marriage would give the Mortimer family a claim to the English throne, as direct descendants of Edward III. During Richard II's troubled and childless reign, in 1385, Parliament declared Roger Mortimer V (1374-98), Earl of March and Ulster, to

Mortimer's Cross

be heir-apparent to the English throne. Roger had married Eleanor Holland, Richard II's niece, a further alliance of the Mortimers with the royal family, but he was killed in Ireland at the age of thirty-seven.

Roger's son, Edmund IV, became the token anti-Lancastrian candidate for those who opposed the usurpation of Henry Bolingbroke in 1399. Bolingbroke had assumed the title and inheritance of the Earls of Hereford through his marriage to Mary Bohun, daughter of the last Earl Humphrey. This made him a prominent landowner in Wales and the Marches, around and beyond Herefordshire and, as such, a dangerous rival to the Mortimers. In the crucial year of Bolingbroke's successful bid for the throne, however, the Mortimer claimant was only eight years old, ward of Henry of Monmouth, Prince of Wales. When Henry IV defeated Hotspur's rebels at Shrewsbury in 1403, Edmund Mortimer was taken to the battlefield at the age of twelve. An abortive rebellion in the summer of 1415 named Mortimer, now 14 years old, as Henry V's rightful successor. The plot was organised by the Plantagenet Earl of Cambridge, Mortimer's brother-in-law and founder of the royal house of York. The Earl of March, however, revealed the plot to Henry V and was pardoned when his supporters were hanged.

Wigmore — village street

Although Edmund Mortimer continued to support Henry V, fighting loyally in France and Wales and suffering repeated imprisonment by Glendower, he was banished to Ireland by Henry VI. With his early death without heirs at 24 years of age, the Mortimer dynasty came to an end. The political influence of their alliance with York lasted longer. In 1461, the grandson of Richard Earl of Cambridge and Anne Mortimer, Edmund Mortimer's great-nephew, became the Yorkist king, Edward IV. He defeated his Lancastrian opponents at Mortimers Cross, near Aymestrey, in Herefordshire. At last the alliance of Mortimer and York had defeated the house of Lancaster.

'The Wars of the Roses', Trevelyan wrote, 'were to a large extent a quarrel among Marcher lords.' Of those great barons, by far the most powerful had been the leaders of the house of Mortimer, of the honour of Wigmore.

IX Medieval Monasteries

*Seal of
Leominster
Priory*

There are no well-preserved monastic sites in Herefordshire. This gives a misleading picture of a county where, throughout the Middle Ages, two dozen communities of monks, nuns and friars represented no fewer than 11 religious orders. Throughout the 12th and 13th centuries 'the religious' colonised the county's frontier. There, away from the rich bishops' manors of the eastern plain, it was impossible to travel more than 10 miles without encountering a religious house and its farms.

Many of these sites, as at Kilpeck, Livers Ocle, Bosbury and Clifford, survive as 17th-century priory farms, the profitable results of the 16th-century dissolution. Imposing medieval crucked houses overlook the rich farmlands of the 'poor nuns' of Limebrook, giving their names to many a Lady Meadow (as at Much Cowarne and Burton), Nun Field (at Berrington and Aston), Nun House (at Eardisland) and Nunsland (Pembridge). On some important sites, such as Wigmore and Flanesford, farmyards surround an isolated but relatively intact monastic building now used as barn, sheepfold or farmhouse. Fish on Friday is recalled by the dry banks of fishponds at Clifford and Wormsley; a few churches like Aconbury retain fragments of earlier communal buildings embedded in their walls. The Knights Templar, a crusading order, have also left their mark. At Harewood Park there are no signs of buildings and Temple Court at Bosbury is now a 17th-century moated manor house, but in the parish church of St Michael, Garway, the circular nave of a typical Templars' church has been traced.

*Seal of
Abbey Dore*

The earliest foundations in the county were the original Mercian minsters. Bromyard was occupied *c*.840 and Leominster was first founded by King Merewald in 660. Destroyed by the Danes, Leominster was re-established as a nunnery in the ninth century but suppressed in 1046 as a result of a notorious scandal involving the abbess with Earl weyn. The priory was revived yet again by Henry I in 1125. Vestiges of the rere-dorter range, the infirmary and the prior's lodging can be seen at Priory House.

Another group of ancient religious houses clustered within the city of Hereford and at its walls. Here were a Benedictine priory, two friaries (one of black, the other of grey friars) and a commandery of the Hospitallers. Of these, the oldest foundation was the priory.

Within the castle's precincts was an older collegiate church, dedicated to St Guthlac, a pre-Conquest foundation. At some time during Robert of Bethune's bishopric (1131-48), the two houses of SS Peter and Guthlac were amalgamated and removed to a site outside the city wall. There are no remains of its buildings and the site is now occupied by a hospital and a bus station.

Arms of St John of Jerusalem

The city's friaries were 13th-century foundations. The Dominican house, reputedly founded by William Cantelupe *c.*1246, had removed from its original site from St Owens Gate to Widemarsh, where its cloisters stand near a rare 14th-century preaching cross, symbol of the mendicant friars. The Grey Friars foundation of 1228, like the Dominicans, is marked on early maps of the city, standing outside Friars Gate. There are no surviving buildings, only the street names at Friar Street and Greyfriars Bridge. Part of the 13th-century commandery of the Hospitallers, east of Widemarsh Street, is concealed within the 17th-century almshouses built by Thomas Coningsby.

In the Herefordshire countryside, the Conquest introduced several cells of foreign abbeys favoured by the Norman conquerors. These were the alien priories of Titley, cell of the French abbey of Tiron; of Monkland, where the Tosnys established an outpost of their family foundations at Conches; and of Livers Ocle, which took its name as a cell of the FitzOsbern abbey of Lyre. The Mortimers were prominent monastic supporters; their greatest house was near Wigmore, where the founders' descendants were buried for several generations. An Augustinian foundation, Wigmore was manned by French canons from St Victor's Abbey near Paris. This, with Abbey Dore, was one of the most substantial monasteries in Herefordshire. Wigmore was well recorded in its own 14th-century chronicle, now far from home in Chicago University.

Monasteries to the west of the county, continually beset by Welsh raiders, relied upon the protection of nearby castles for knightly protection. At Clifford, the route of the relief column is still known as Succour Lane. Later, the Talbots favoured the Augustinians at Flanesford and Wormsley, just as the Lacys and Mortimers enriched their sister houses at Aconbury and Limebrook. There, a lady of the baronial family might turn to a contemplative life, occasionally as prioress, and there was an interchange of sisters from house to house.

Column head, Priory church, Leominster

The regular orders of the Catholic church played an ever-present part in the religious, social and economic life of medieval Hereford-shire, providing employment and welfare services in many a village. Discipline was hard to maintain in the smaller isolated cells, and visitations tell familiar tales of scandalous behaviour bringing

53

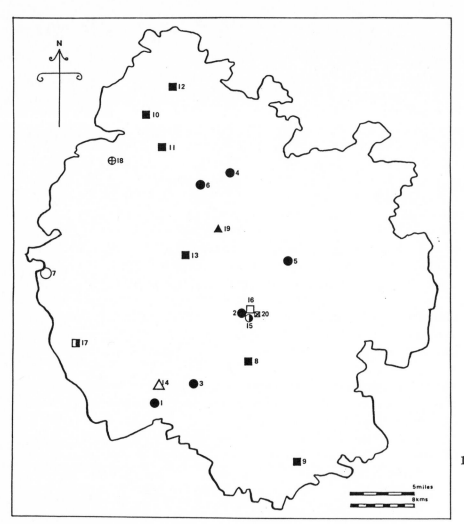

11. Medieval Monasteries.

Benedictine Order:

1. Ewyas Harold. Priory of Ss James and Bartholomew
   (Fr: Harold of Ewyas, c.1100-1359)
2. Hereford Priory of St Guthlac
   (Fr: Hugh de Lacy, 1101-1538)
3. Kilpeck. Priory of St David
   (Fr: Hugh Fitzwilliam, 1134-1540)
4. Leominster. Priory of Ss Peter & Paul
   (Fr: Henry I, 1125-1539)
5. Livers Ocle alien cell (1100-c.1414)
6. Monkland, alien cell (Before 1100-c.1414)

Cluniac Order:

7. Clifford. alien Cluniac Priory of St Mary
   (Fr: Simon FitzRichard, c.1129-1536)

Augustinian Canons (*) and Canonesses (**):

8. (**) Aconbury. Priory of Holy Cross and St Catherine
   (Fr: Lady Margery Lacy, c.1207-1539)
9. (*) Flanesford. Priory of St John the Baptist
   (Fr: Sir Richard Talbot, 1346-1536)
10. (**) Limebrook. Priory of St Mary
    (Frs: ?Mortimer or de Lingen family, c1189-1539)
11. (*) Shobdon. Priory of St John the Evangelist
    (Fr: Oliver de Merlimond, c.1140-c.1172)
12. (*) Wigmore. Abbey of St James
    (Fr: Hugh I of Mortimer, c.1172-1538)
13. (*) Wormsley. Priory of Ss Mary and Leonard
    (Fr: Gilbert Talbot, after 1200-1539)

Cistercian Order:

14. Abbey Dore. Abbey of St Mary
    (Fr: Robert de Ewyas, 1147-1536)

Dominican or Black Friars:

15. Hereford. Dedication unknown
    (Fr: ? William Cantilupe, c.1246-1538)

Franciscan or Grey Friars:

16. Hereford. Dedication unknown
    (Fr: Sir William Pembrugge, before 1228-1538)

Grandmontine Order:

17. Craswall alien Priory
    (c.1225-1462)

Tironensian Congregation:

18. Titley, alien cell
    (1221-1391)

Knights Hospitallers of St John of Jerusalem:

19. Commandery of Dinmore
    (Fr: Thomas de Dunmore, c.1163-1540)

Knights Templars:

20. Preceptory of Hereford

monasteries into disrepute. The dissolute life of the tiny community at Ewias Harold in 1359 caused the Abbot of Gloucester to withdraw the prior and his two monks, letting the priory's income revert to the support of the parish church, which also gained a tower from the suppressed priory.

England's continual wars with France caused patriotic reaction against alien priories. Between 1391 and 1462 these were suppressed and their property given to schools and colleges. The pattern was set for Henry VIII's dissolution of the major houses between 1536 and 1539. Small houses like Flanesford, reduced to poverty by plague, hard times and mismanagement were among the first to go. Abbey Dore, subject to constant border raids, was, in spite of trade in wool and timber, 'greatly in ruin and decay' by 1536. As a result of the intercession of the Earl of Shrewsbury and his payment of a fine of £200, the hardworking priory of Wormsley was spared 'in perpetuity' – in fact, until 1539. In defence of Aconbury, even a reforming bishop could acknowledge that there, 'women and children were brought up in virtue and learning'. The house was dissolved in 1539.

Apart from their scanty ruins, quarries of building stone for ages, and some dry fishponds, the legacy of Herefordshire monasteries was a new class of landlord and many rare books. The Chronicle of Wigmore, the manuscripts of Limebrook, the libraries of the Franciscans at Hereford and the Cistercians at Abbey Dore – these are their only permanent records, apart from place-names like Brampton Abbots, Nunsland, Temple Court and Friar Street.

Chained library, Hereford

Misericord — Hereford Cathedral

X The City of Hereford

*Hereford City
Arms*

Hereford was the first Saxon *burh* to be planted west of the Severn, a planned town, founded by King Mildfrith in the seventh century. By 930 its mint was making coins for King Aethelstan of Wessex. The ramparts of the Saxon town are clearly marked in the streets around the cathedral. In the north, an earthen bank and timber palisade bent along *Behyndthewall Lane* (now Packers Lane) to meet St Owens Street, and continued to the river at the castle ford. The western defences ran from Little Packers Lane via Eign Gate to the river again at Wye Bridge. An outlying ditch, thrown up on the south side of the river (possibly in the ninth century), was later named Row Ditch. A small section of this Saxon rampart is exposed to view on the corner of Mill Street, behind a block of newly-built redbrick flats.

The Saxon town covered about 25 acres, divided by an interior 'King's Ditch' between the *civitas* of earl and king and the bishop's *port*. The minster was enlarged by Bishop Aethelstan in 1040 and Earl Ralf of Mantes built a castle there before the Conquest. By this time the street plan of the centre of Hereford was fixed for a thousand years. In 1055, the *Chronicle* records a Welsh invasion, when the Cathedral was plundered. Later that year, Harold Godwinsson arrived with an army from Gloucester and threw up a stronger earthwork around the town. According to Domesday, 'In the city of Hereford before 1066, there were 103 families dwelling inside and outside the wall'. There were six smiths in Norman Hereford, each making 120 royal horse-shoes at 3d. each. Of the city's seven coiners, one belonged to the bishop. In the *port*, however, where once 98 houses had stood, there were now only 60 and the new French bishop, Robert of Lorraine, found 40 hides laid waste. It was either Earl Harold or his Norman successor FitzOsbern who enlarged the boundary of the medieval city to the north. The extension lay on both sides of Widemarsh Street and Bye Street, making room for a new market-place, with 'rows' for butchers, cooks, mercers, drapers, fishmongers and leather-workers and streets for Jews and 'Frenschemenne'. There were now six gates in the walls and a dry-bridge over Row Ditch, beyond Wye Bridge Gate. The extent of the medieval town was about 93 acres.

*Cherub and date,
Old House,
Hereford*

Hereford's fine series of charters begins in 1189, when Richard I offered the citizens an annual rent of £40 and made them exempt from

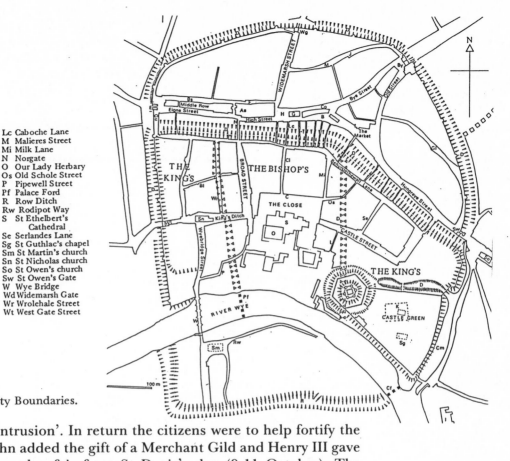

A Aley
As All Saints church
B Butchery
Bl Black Lane
Bs Bewel Street
By Bye Street Gate
C Canons Street
Cf Castle Ford
Cl Caboche Lane
Cm Castle Moat
Co Coken Row
D Ditch
E Eign Gate
F Frenchemanne
  Street
G Gildhall
Gl Grope Lane
Gu Guildeforde Street
H High Town
I Infirmary
J Jews Street
K Kings Palace?
L Little Lane

Lc Caboche Lane
M Malieres Street
Mi Milk Lane
N Norgate
O Our Lady Herbary
Os Old Schole Street
P Pipewell Street
Pf Palace Ford
R Row Ditch
Rw Rodipot Way
S St Ethelbert's
  Cathedral
Se Serlandes Lane
Sg St Guthlac's chapel
Sm St Martin's church
Sn St Nicholas church
So St Owen's church
Sw St Owen's Gate
W Wye Bridge
Wd Widemarsh Gate
Wr Wrolehale Street
Wt West Gate Street

12. Hereford City Boundaries.

the sheriff's 'intrusion'. In return the citizens were to help fortify the town. King John added the gift of a Merchant Gild and Henry III gave an annual three-day fair from St Denis's day (9-11 October). The bishop already had a fair, granted in 1121 by Henry I.

In 1298, Edward I's charter gave a *murage* grant of five years' tolls on woad, onions and garlic to pay for the repair of the walls. These were now 2350 feet long, with 17 semi-circular stone bastions, each 20 feet tall. Edward I's conquest of Wales reduced the importance of Hereford castle, but encouraged the growth of peaceful trade. A flourishing cloth industry was established, with 20 gilds for tailors, cappers, hosiers, dyers, fullers and weavers. The Dean and Chapter's ovens also promoted a profitable export of bread into Wales and, with their own fulling mills, the churchmen contributed to the prosperity of the city. In spite of recurrent plague in 1348 and 1361, the city's medieval wealth is reflected in the continuous 14th-century embellishment of the cathedral. Richard II permitted Sit John Burley, Hereford's Bailiff, to take the title of Mayor and offered the burgesses a site for their court-house.

Ironically, incorporation 'as a body politic' was granted by Elizabeth I in 1597, just as the city was going into a long decline.

Hereford Cathedral – from Speed's map of 1610

Before the charter took effect there was already a growing need to set unemployed clothiers to work and John Speed's map of Hereford in 1610 shows little suburban development beyond the medieval gates. Hereford's impoverishment began with the Reformation, which stole the city's religious wealth, and continued during the civil war, which ruined its trade. Yet, at this time, several of the city's finest timber houses were built, including the Market House and the Guildhall. The 17th century is notable for the charitable foundation of several Hospitals in Hereford – Kenning's, William's, Coningesby's and the Weavers' – but these could not contain the growing problem of the aged poor, the unemployed and 'sturdy beggars' on the streets.

During the 18th century, the city's prosperity depended on the glovers' trade. During this time, there was a wealth of public benefaction which produced an impressive array of new buildings in brick. These include the Bluecoat School (1710); Mary Shelley's Hospital (1710); Congregational Church (1740); Guildhall (1759); Infirmary (1793); County Gaol (1793); Lunatic Asylum (1794); and the Countess of Huntingdon's Chapel and the Wesleyan Chapel, both built in 1796. Hereford was no longer a half-timbered city.

Taylor's map of 1757 is exactly co-extensive with Speed's. He tabulates 1279 houses for 5592 inhabitants. Of these 812 houses were within the walls, accommodating 3816 people; 467 were outside, for 1776 inhabitants. According to Taylor, the environs of the city were sylvan, with the cathedral spire still rising above the trees, before its demolition in 1794/5.

St Owen's Gate, Hereford

Until 1852 Hereford remained much as Taylor had mapped it but, between 1854 and 1865, the streets beyond the gates were built up with particular developments around the northern wall on New Market Street. The area towards Bartonsham, too, was laid out with new terraces round Park Street and Harold Street. Intermittent growth continued from 1870 to 1900, with peaks of street building in 1878, 1883 and 1891. This period saw new housing along Whitecross Street for more than a mile beyond Eign Gate. Similar development took place around New Town Road and by Barrs Court Railway Station. Building continued as the population grew towards 50,000, especially between the wars, in the estates around Hinton. Hereford has outgrown its medieval walls across a four-mile circle. Fossilized at the centre, still clearly marked by walls and gates, is the ancient cathedral city.

58

XI The Ancient Boroughs

Leominster's position, after Hereford, is exceptional from the time of Domesday, when it was a vast complex of royal manors. From 1125, the town was dominated by Henry I's priory, a cell of Reading's Benedictine abbey. The abbots had extensive jurisidiction over the town, controlling its privileges, appointing its bailiffs and often alienating the burgesses. The original town was to the west of the present site, by Vicarage Street, with an entrenchment along School Lane. Leominster was continually attacked; Welsh princes and Norman lords all took their toll. By 1235, Leominster's market challenged Hereford and Worcester. The town's wealth was in the excellence of its wool, the 'Lempster Ore'. Edward I granted the town two fairs and a seal, and summoned two burgesses to his Parliaments. During the Lancastrian reign, Herefordshire was a notorious centre of heresy and political opposition and Leominster was the centre of unrest. Opposition to the Lancastrians was supported by the revolt of Owen Glendower, a dominant influence in the north of Herefordshire. Glendower invaded the county, defeated Edward Mortimer, captured Leominster, occupied the hill-site of Ivington and plundered the priory. During the Wars of the Roses, the town successfully supported the Yorkist cause.

Leland described Leominster during Henry VIII's reign as 'metely large, with good buildings of timber'. There were eight gilds, of butchers, bakers, cordwainers, glovers, mercers, tailors, tanners and fullers, who helped maintain the town's 10 bridges. The priory was dissolved in 1539 and the abbot was hanged at Reading. The dissolution endowed the grammar school, successor to three medieval chantries, but this was attached to the parochial school in 1860. In 1554 the Tudor Queen gave the town its charter of incorporation 'because they did valiantly withstand the said late Duke and his confederates, who to us were most troublesome'. The citizens now enjoyed municipality in their own right. Under Elizabeth I, Leominster was once more a revolutionary place, dissenting in religion. In 1610 a recusant priest, Roger Cadwallader, was tried and executed at Leominster Assizes. During the Commonwealth Leominster became a 'little Amsterdam' of Baptists and Presbyterians, and the Quaker centre of Herefordshire.

St Michael and All Angels — late 12th-century detached bell tower

59

17th-century Abbotts Lodge and Church House

Leominster's wool trade declined after the Restoration, but the borough continued to send two members to Parliament until 1885. A poll-list of 1780 lists 396 voters with two votes each. Their occupations were mostly in leatherwork, as cordwainers, tanners and glovers, with some weavers and flaxdressers, and a few braziers and tinmen. In the 19th century, Leominster attempted several industrial ventures, like French hat-making and cotton manufacture, but its mainstay, gloving, declined, and by 1830 Pigot observed that the town 'appears to be in more of a state of decay than of improvement'.

All Herefordshire's towns were agricultural manors in Domesday – only Wigmore was a borough – but there were several more seigneurial foundations during the Middle Ages. Weobley was founded by the Lacys in 1140 and Henry of Pembridge gave his town a charter in 1241. Richards Castle protected 103 burgesses in 1304 and there were 100 at Ewias Harold. Even small villages like Huntingdon and Stapleton once had burgages, but none survived as towns. Of the rest, the most firmly established were the markets at the gates of the bishop's 'palaces'. Thirteenth-century surveys of the burgages of Ledbury (pop:282), Bromyard (225) and Ross (105) were recorded in the bishops' *Red Book*. These list rents – 1s. for each burgage and 3d. for a stall in the market-places. Streets are named in the bishops' surveys and in 1970 Joseph Hillaby, using the *Red Book* and ancient maps, painted a vivid picture of a well-planned medieval town in Ledbury. The market, granted by Stephen's charter of 1138, was held in Middletown, in the triangle between the Upper and Lower Crosses. This, with its later Middle Row, Butchers' Row and Shop Row, replaced an earlier Saxon market on the village green at Church Lane. Later 13th-century growth is seen in a New Street and the extensions of Homme End, Southende and Bysshopstrete. Medieval trades are evident in the shopkeepers' surnames – the Mercers, Millers, Weavers and Goldsmiths. Population grew during the 13th century but during the later Middle Ages, plagues and recession impoverished the town.

side elevation of Church House

Reformation brought in new men – Skypps, Eltons and Skynners – who profited from sales of church lands. They founded influential families and promoted trade, so that the later 16th century saw a revival of cloth and leather work in Ledbury. The townsmen spent their wealth on the finest range of Jacobean timber-framed buildings in the county and the Hearth Tax returns record a town of 227 houses.

Like Hereford and Leominster, Ledbury's industrial prosperity waned in the 18th century, 'for want of cheap carriage', but the people riotously resisted the turnpike trusts' improvements. Manufacture of broadcloth and silk-weaving declined and Ledbury reverted to its

60

medieval situation as an agricultural market town. Not even an ambitious plan to link Hereford, Ledbury and Birmingham by canal could create an economic revival. By 1830, the produce of orchards and hopyards was the town's staple trade.

St Michael and All Angels

Bromyard was the third in rank of the bishop's boroughs, an early Saxon mission centre. Like Ledbury, its medieval streets and trades are described in the *Red Book*. Here, too, we find medieval burgages, 47 shops and a substantial clothiers' trade. The bounds of the medieval borough and its 'foreign' are still clearly defined by the modern parish boundaries, for, though in the 17th century Bromyard was said to be one of the most ancient market towns in England, the town failed to develop later. Even the opening of the railway in 1878 failed to create industrial expansion; the town's cattle market was its most profitable feature, in Beast Street, Sheep Street, Swine Street and Horse Fair. Even as a farmers' market town, Bromyard declined in the late 19th century. Pigot dismisses the town as having 'neither well-built houses nor regular streets, its whole appearance is far from prepossessing'. In fact, the town is probably busier and more industrious today than it has been for several generations.

Ross is aptly named from the Welsh *rhos* for a hill or promontory. Successor to Roman *Ariconium*, this is an ancient town made in a new image. Here was another of Hereford's medieval bishops' 'palaces' – now the *Royal Hotel* – but, like Bromyard, the borough which the bishops planned was slow to develop and was never incorporated. In Domesday there were no burgages but 27 families with 27 ploughs. Ross's market grew, with nine stalls recorded in the *Red Book* and 96 other burgage tenements at 1s. rent.

front entrance of Abbey House

The town's ruined 'medieval walls' are an illusion, however. These, like the rest of Ross's Gothick image, are a product of the 1830s. Nineteenth-century builders merely followed a tradition of public works, laid down by an earlier town planner. Eighteenth-century Ross was the creation of John Kyrle (1637-1724), Alexander Pope's 'Man of Ross'. Kyrle laid on a water supply, built a causeway to Wilton Bridge, restored the 14th-century church spire which dominates any view of the town and planned the Prospect Gardens. His house is now a shop in the Market Square where the open Market House stands. This is an imposing twin-gabled sandstone building, rebuilt in 1660, standing on an island in the Square. High in the eastern wall is a white stone relief picture of Charles II in full-bottomed wig, another of Kyrle's adornments to the town.

In 1830, Ross was a favourite summer resort and tourist centre. There were four Reading Societies, a Mechanics' Institute, a Horticultural Society with 400 members and a Bluecoat School.

building on five wooden posts, overhanging the pavement

Church Street has several fine Georgian and Regency houses. There was a wide range of 19th-century crafts, though on a small scale. Baskets and rope were made – the Rope Walk survives – and there were small numbers of nailers, flax dressers and weavers, glovers, braziers and woolstaplers. The town's real trade was in the market hall, its 17 inns and a well-stocked street of shops. Later the manufacture of agricultural implements, boots and flour gave employment to a growing population. Nowadays, the town makes farm machinery, plastic mouldings and other modern goods on industrial estates around the abandoned railway station.

Weobley is notable for its deserted medieval castle site, a fine 14th-century church and a wide market place on Broad Street, which lost its ancient Market House and middle row in the 1840s. The medieval town boasted a market, two fairs and even a small Jewry. There is an impressive range of half-timbered town-houses dating from the Middle Ages. These have many exceptional features, such as the massive medieval crucks of a small house, once a honeymoon cottage, in the *Red Lion's* yard and a dragon-beam on the corner of the inn itself, which divides the jetties over both streets. Almost every kind of timber stud, post and panel can be found in Weobley's houses.

In 1533, Leland described Weobley as 'a market town where there is a goodly castle, but somewhat in decay'. There are 17th-century weavers' inventories from Weobley, but the town's chief manufacture was ale. Camden said that Weobley had 'more fair cellars than most market towns of its bigness in England' but 'with the increase for syder, this commodity hath declined'. In the 1830s, Pigot's *Directory* refers to a 'principal manufacture' of nails and malt. His list of shops included seven tailors, six butchers, a watch and clock-maker and a druggist, 'several shops having been opened in a very spirited manner'. The 1830s, however, were the days of Weobley's greatest notoriety as one of the 56 Parliamentary 'rotten' and 'pocket' boroughs disenfranchised by the Reform Act of 1832.

As an 'ancient borough', Weobley had sent two members to Parliament from 1295 to 1306 but their franchise, like that of Bromyard, Ledbury and Ross, then lapsed. In 1628, the Tomkyns family, owners of the Garnstone estate and MPs for Leominster, successfully petitioned Parliament for Weobley's re-enfranchisement. For the next 100 years, the elections were contested successively by five local families – the Tomkyns and Birches from Garnstone, the Prices of Foxley, the Cornewalls of Moccas and Berrington and the Foleys of Stoke Edith, newcomers from the Black Country.

The asking price of a vote might be a pair of new shoes, 'entertainments', a guinea – or threats. In 1717, Thomas Foley paid

62

out £700 for a by-election which he lost because Weobley voters were reliable only 'unless someone spent more money on them ...'. In 1754, Weobley's parliamentary seats became virtually the property of the Thynne family from Wiltshire who, as lords of the manor, bought up the majority of the town's burgage tenements. Weobley was, from 1754 to 1832, a typical 'pocket borough'. In 1832, the Whigs' first Reform Act took both members from every borough with fewer than 2,000 voters, giving Herefordshire an extra seat in compensation for Weobley's two members.

By 1795 a local guide-book described a town in decay: 'Weobley consists of a few small streets meanly constructed, without either market or traffic to establish its title to the rank of a town'. Road-books describe Broad Street as 'ankle deep in mud and furrowed as if by a plough-share'. By the second half of the 19th century, all Weobley's small crafts, like nailing and glove-making, were gone. The Tan House was closed and a short-lived cattle fair was discontinued for want of trade. Yet, by 1899, the town had a piped water supply and oil lamps for street-lighting. Today the town has a small industrial estate and many other busy enterprises. Like many of Herefordshire's ancient towns, reports of Weobley's demise were perhaps, in the end, exaggerated.

Ledbury Park

XII Lords and Ladies

*Lady in
wimple
(Wolferlow)*

Herefordshire is rich in monumental effigies. A few, worn and defaced, have survived from the 13th century; many more are of a later date. These effigies invite conjecture about the motives of those who commissioned them. Some, no doubt, wished merely to show off their wealth, with the same extravagance that they displayed in building closely-studded timber-framed houses, or wore their wealth on their backs. A few are evidently expressions of family affection and filial respect. Some sought to impress posterity; all looked for immortality.

For students of costume, these effigies provide not only textbook examples of aristocratic fashion in each generation but also human touches. Sometimes the small detail of a simple tomb makes it memorable. In Bodenham, for example, we examine the coif and wimple of the 14th-century woman who lies under an arch in the chancel, then our eye is drawn to the hand she gives to a child hidden in the fold of her mother's mantle. The tomb of a 14th-century Knight of the Garter, Sir William Pembridge of Clehonger, shows him in ridged bascinet, scalloped mail hauberk and rich surcoat. Near him a gentler figure lies in a tight-fitting gown with hip-belt and buttoned sleeves, her long hair bound with a fillet. Over all, she wears a long cloak, her only ornament a buckled necklace. At her feet a large goose pulls at her cloak with its beak.

At Edvin Ralf there are more 14th-century effigies. Here, the women are simply dressed in long gown with tight sleeves and veiled head-dresses. These are less ornate than those of the same period in Welsh Bicknor church, where a lady wears a barbe-and-coif head-dress; her dress has tight sleeves under a heavily draped gown. In her left hand she holds a ribbon, looped to the shoulder of her dress. This is believed to be Margaret Montacute, wife of Sir John, whose father brought the boy-king Edward III to the throne.

One of the most interesting 15th-century altar tombs is at Kington. A knight, in plate armour, with breast-plate articulated in the Gothic fashion, collared with suns and roses, rests his head on a helm, his feet on a lion. This is Thomas Vaughan, slain at Banbury in 1469. His wife, with clasped hands and a meek expression, belies her reputation as Ellen the Terrible. The legend is that in order to avenge her

21. Leominster Market Place *c.* 1830. This painting by John Scarlett Davis (1804–44) shows the old timbered Market Hall which is now rebuilt as Grange Court, the District Council offices near the church.

22. The timber market hall at Pembridge, which Cassey's Directory for 1858 described as 'formerly a market town', with two fairs for livestock and hiring in May and November.

23. The elegant 17th-century figures of Sir John Kyrle and his wife in Much Marcle church display the height of Cavalier fashion, in his long hair, ruff, armour and embroidered sash and her brocaded gown with slashed sleeves.

24. Unknown members of the Unett family, in the chancel of Castle Frome church, with their nine children kneeling around them.

25. 'Roaring Meg', the great Parliamentarian mortar which bombarded Goodrich Castle during the siege of 1646. This striking monument of the Civil War in Herefordshire now stands in Churchill Gardens, Hereford.

26. Colonel John Birch's controversial monument in Weobley church. The inscription describes him as 'Vindicating the Laws and Liberties of his country in War and promoting its Welfare and Prosperity in Peace'.

27. The outstanding Norman font at St Michael's church at Castle Frome is an eminent example of the work of the 'Herefordshire school', which made similar fonts at Shobdon, Eardisley, and, in Worcestershire, at Chaddesley Corbett. Carved from old red sandstone (*c.* 1140), with a diameter of 4½ ft., the bowl stands on three crouching creatures; it depicts the Baptism of Christ with symbols of the Evangelists. The base is said to suggest experience of Italian art.

brother's death, she attended an archery contest disguised as a man and killed his murderer with an arrow through the heart.

In the chancel of Burghill church, the 15th-century alabaster effigies of Sir John Milbourne and his wife Elizabeth show fine detail of armour and costume. Sir John seems overweight, either by armour or devotion. Elizabeth's gown, with close-fitting bodice, sur-coat and horned head-dress, is complemented by her lovely necklace and heart-shaped locket. It is sad to see her broken arms and the battered condition of the nine children at the end of the tomb.

The helmet on the effigy of a 14th-century knight (Much Marcle)

In only a few Herefordshire churches are the medieval memorials recorded in brass instead of stone. The finest of these are to be found in the cathedral, particularly the brass of Richard and Isabella Delamere, who died in 1435 and 1421 respectively. The lady wears a tight, backless over-gown with liripipe sleeves and a heart-shaped, padded head-dress. Her husband is dressed in Lancastrian armour. Of other brasses, that in Marden of Dame Margaret Chute is noteworthy. Her regal figure in fine lace collar and long skirt is crowned by a many-pointed head-dress. The human touch is added once again in the tiny replica, by her side, of her daughter Ann, who died with her mother on the day she was born.

The county's outstanding 16th-century memorial is undoubtedly the beautifully coloured altar tomb of Alexander Denton (*d.*1576) and his wife Anne (*d.*1566), which stands in the south transept of the cathedral. The short-haired, bearded figure of this Elizabethan gentleman lies in decorated plate armour, wearing a heavy double chain and cross, gauntlets at his side, his head on a crested helm, his feet on a lion. Ann Denton, aged 17, wears a closely fitting gown with a high collar and the small ruff and puffed shoulders of the period. From her girdle hangs a jewelled pendant; by her side, wrapped in the folds of her skirt, lies her newly-born child, in swaddling bands. Ann was another casualty of Tudor child-birth.

Possibly the most unusual Elizabethan monument is found at Bacton, which has a rare portrayal of the Queen herself. The memorial commemorates Blanche Parry, maid-of-honour to Elizabeth I. Blanche kneels beside the Queen, who is crowned and wearing the familiar close-fitting corsage, its high collar encrusted with jewels. The two figures are set in an impressive arched recess, flanked by Corinthian columns.

Clasped hands (John Rudhall's tomb: Ross, 1636)

In Holme Lacy church the monuments of the Scudamores record an impressive family history. Of particular note is that of Sir John Scudamore, in 1571, and his wife Sibell. He wears 16th-century armour; his hands, folded in prayer, neglect the sword at his left side and the gauntlet at his right; he wears a double chain around his neck.

Blanche Perry

John's fashion-conscious wife wears a long gown with a pedimented head-dress; her praying hands still hold her gloves.

Much Marcle is rich in monuments from the 14th to the 17th century. Here is the later 14th-century Grandison tomb (*c.*1360-70) of Blanche, daughter of Roger Mortimer of Wigmore, first Earl of March, and wife of Sir Peter Grandison, lord of the manor. Her decorated floral head-band is especially attractive; her left hand holds a rosary. Blanche is portrayed, in medieval tradition, as aged about 30, the age of Christ at His Resurrection. Dominating the chapel on their altar-tomb of black marble lie Sir John and Lady Kyrle (1650). She wears a crimped ruff and veil. John has a long falling collar and a sash decorated with fleurs-de-lys. His feet rest on a realistic little hedgehog, later the emblem on Ross's seal.

Not all the Herefordshire effigies are of the gentry. In contrast, also at Much Marcle, lies a rare 14th-century painted oak figure. Here we see Walter de Hellen, who served the Audley family as their steward. He is dressed in a close-fitting, buttoned jerkin of russet cloth which reaches to his knees. His tight sleeves are also buttoned from wrist to elbow and his hip-belt carries a sword, with his purse on the right side. This solemn, bearded man was a franklin or landed gentleman.

The county's 17th-century effigies are outstanding, both in number and quality. That of another John Scudamore, at Kentchurch (1616) is remarkable for the figures' unusual reclining posture and the standing small-scale figures of their eight sons and a daughter, who show fashionable clothes in miniature. Husband and wife hold Bibles and she wears her widow's veil. John's elegant breeches are typical of early Jacobean fashion. The Unett monument at Castle Frome (1624) is another outstanding model. Sir William wears Cavalier dress and seems to have stepped from a picture by Van Dyck, with his full sashed sleeves, breeches with ribboned points and boot hose-tops. Left hand on breast, Bible clasped in the right and lowered eyes speak of a devout attitude to life and death. John's wife's dress is simply draped. Their nine children kneel at the base of the tomb, each carrying a Bible.

The memorial of a similar date (1636) in Ross church, to John Rudhall's family, present children in less formal attitudes. The Rudhall monument, almost identical in fashion to the later Kyrle effigies described above, conveys a loving family picture. It is touching to see John and his wife seeking immortality hand-in-hand. The wealth of their apparel seems of secondary importance to this portrayal of their affection and trust.

XIII The Country Houses

The stately homes of Herefordshire have a character of their own. The county cannot boast a Blenheim Palace or Castle Howard; instead, it contains many comfortable, distinguished homes. Manor houses, or Courts as they are locally named, can be found to illustrate styles of English architecture from the 14th to the 20th centuries. Hereford-shire is fortunate in possessing at least three outstanding examples of 14th-century hall-houses. These are at Burton Court in Eardisland, hidden behind a neo-Tudor front; at Wellbrook Manor, Peterchurch, a most notable example; and at Brinsop, where there is a moated manor-house in fine condition.

National Trust emblem

There are fewer exposed large timber-framed houses of the Elizabethan and Jacobean periods than one might have expected from the Herefordshire gentry, though more are concealed behind later buildings. Outstanding among the survivors are Luntley Court in Dilwyn, the Tomkyns house, and Hall Court at Much Marcle. Ledbury Court, built in the 16th century by the Hall family, is a grand timber town house with five gables. Also worthy of note are the black-and-white houses of Wythall, Walford-on-Wye and the H-shaped Freens Court at Sutton, formerly the seat of the Unetts. Other 17th-century buildings are in varying condition. At Eye Manor, the plaster ceilings are of a high quality, and Weston Hall at Weston-under-Penyard is a fine example of a Jacobean house.

Regrettably, many fine Herefordshire houses have been lost. Victorian restorers of the Jacobean Fownhope Court succeeded only in virtually destroying the original. Between 1948 and 1958, 18 notable houses were demolished, including Aramstone House at King's Caple, which was said to be the most important Georgian house in the county. Garnstone, at Weobley, a house designed by Nash on the site of Colonel Birch's home, was also pulled down in 1959. Fire, too, has taken its toll of several mansions, including, in 1927, the Foleys' fine house in Stoke Edith Park.

Some of the county's houses have not suffered such violent change, however. Homme House at Much Marcle, for example, is as serene and private today as when Francis Kilvert described, in his diary for September 1874, the wedding of his friend Revd. Andrew Pope to Miss Harriet Money-Kyrle, at which Kilvert was best man. After the

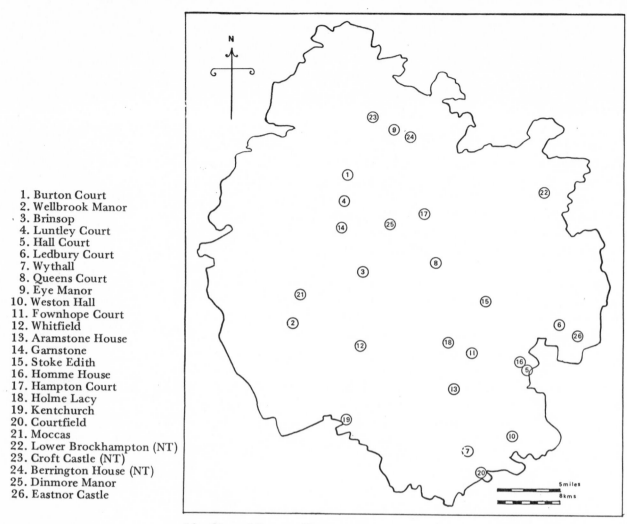

1. Burton Court
2. Wellbrook Manor
3. Brinsop
4. Luntley Court
5. Hall Court
6. Ledbury Court
7. Wythall
8. Queens Court
9. Eye Manor
10. Weston Hall
11. Fownhope Court
12. Whitfield
13. Aramstone House
14. Garnstone
15. Stoke Edith
16. Homme House
17. Hampton Court
18. Holme Lacy
19. Kentchurch
20. Courtfield
21. Moccas
22. Lower Brockhampton (NT)
23. Croft Castle (NT)
24. Berrington House (NT)
25. Dinmore Manor
26. Eastnor Castle

13. Sites of Country Houses.

wedding breakfast, he writes,'we were all photographed on the steps before the house'.

Change of ownership of other houses reflects new patterns in the county's social structure. For example, John Arkwright, grandson of Sir Richard, the Lancashire industrialist who invented the spinning-frame, bought Hampton Court, the largest medieval manor-house in England, which he transformed in the 1830s. In the present century there is no longer a Scudamore at Holme Lacy House, which is now a hospital, though members of the family still live at Kentchurch Court. There is a school at Courtfield, home of the Vaughans, and the name of Cornewall has gone from Moccas.

68

The six houses described in this chapter are chosen from those which welcome visitors during the summer season. In some instances, not only the houses, but their gardens as well, make a visit memorable. A distinguished medieval example is the remote 14th-century timber-framed manor-house at Lower Brockhampton. Here the moat still surrounds three sides of the house, re-emphasising its defensive position even today. The exposed timber framing is partly in square posts and panels, partly in close upright studs. The bargeboards on the gables are elaborately decorated. Much of the western wing of the original H-shaped building was rebuilt in the 16th and 17th centuries, but two bays of the Great Hall survive. An outstanding feature at Brockhampton is the detached gatehouse on the moat, one of the few in existence. It was built in the later 15th century, a small square house, with a jettied upper storey, projecting on curved brackets. The upright studding is close-set and ostentatious for its period. An open archway runs through the building, with an interior gate and staircase. The bargeboards on the gable ends are ornately decorated with a leaf motif. Nearby are the ruins of a 12th-century chapel. Now the property of the National Trust, Brockhampton Manor belonged since the 16th century to the Barneby and Lutley families. It is one of the county's many exceptional buildings.

Near the turbulent Welsh border, below the massive hill-fort of Croft Ambrey, stands Croft Castle, described by John Leland in 1538 as, 'sett on the browe of a hill, somewhat rokky, dychid and waulled, castle-like'. The Castle has remained in the hands of one family longer than any other great house in Herefordshire. The Domesday tenant, Bernard, held Croft, Wharton and Newton from William d'Ecouis, and was succeeded by Hugh 'de Croft'. Croft was originally a Marcher castle, and, during the Civil War, a Royalist stronghold. Its plan is on a roughly square court-yard, with a tower in each corner. Medieval masonry now blends with newer parapets and sash windows, set in Gothic bays.

In 1956 the building was preserved for the public, with the assistance of the Ministry of Works and the National Trust. Inside the house are many Gothic features, added in the mid-18th-century style by the Knight family, wealthy Shropshire iron-masters. A sense of successive generations, each making its contribution, is enhanced by 17th-century panelling and chimney-piece in the Oak Room and 18th-century decoration of the drawing-room. The grand staircase, too, with its elaborate plaster-work, the details of the ceiling panels in the Blue Room and the painted bookcases in the library are a fitting background to a collection of Gothic furniture. Near the castle is the

Lower Brockhampton House — timber framed gatehouse

*Sir Richard and
Dame Eleanor Croft*

church, with the 16th-century altar tomb of Sir Richard Croft and his wife. The park-land surrounding castle and church contains some of the finest oaks in England and a 300-year-old avenue of sweet chestnuts almost half a mile long. In contrast to these tall trees are the drifts of pink and white cyclamen which border the drive, making a memorable picture in their season.

A member of the Cornewall family originally held the Berrington estate at Eye, a more senior branch than those at Moccas Court. Berrington was built in the 18th century by Thomas Harley of Brampton Bryan, Lord Mayor of London, and was completed in 1701. Through the Harley's female line the house became the property of George, son of Admiral Lord Rodney, well-rewarded victor of the Battle of the Saints in 1782. Many of the paintings of interest in the house depict the Admiral's naval actions. Berrington's drawing-room is outstanding for its ceiling alone. Designed by Holland, in lavender and gold, its fine medallions show a strong Italian influence. The elegant furniture is French, with a set of 19th-century gilt settee and chairs upholstered in French tapestry. Unlike many houses spoiled by restoration, the beauty of Berrington House's interior has remained unaltered since 1780. In 1901, Berrington House was sold to Frederick Cawley, MP for Prestwich in Lancashire. Still the house remained in the Cawley family's ownership until 1957 when it became the property of the National Trust. The then dowager Lady Cawley remained a tenant until her death in 1978 at the age of 101. Her room preserves a touching collection of family memorabilia.

There has been a house on the site of Moccas Court since the 13th century. The estate became the property of Edward Cornewall of Berrington when he married Frances, widow of Henry Vaughan, in 1650. The present house was built in 1775 to the design of Robert and James Adam. It is of mellow red brick with a plain elevation. An attractive feature of the house is a central Venetian window; the rounded porch below this was added in 1792. The lodges at the park gates were built at the beginning of the 19th century. Both Capability Brown and Humphry Repton were involved in landscaping the park. Sir George Cornewall, who is frequently mentioned in Kilvert's diary, was rector of the church across the park for 40 years. The trees which Kilvert admired still stand today. 'They look', wrote Kilvert, 'as if they had been at the beginning and making of the world and they will probably see its end.'

Berrington Hall

In 1916 Sir William Cornewall, last unmarried owner to bear the name, moved to a smaller house on the estate; in 1946, he sold the furniture and contents. The present owner, whose father inherited the estate from Sir William, came to Moccas in 1962. Gradually the house is being re-furnished, sometimes with its original furniture.

The Cornewalls were a musical family and the father of the first Sir George was a friend of Handel and executor of his estate. It is said that music could always be heard in the house. In the old music room, there is a gilded frieze of musical instruments; more decorate the marble chimney-piece. Curved mahogany doors lead from the now depleted library (3,000 books went into the sale) into a remarkable circular drawing-room, designed by Robert Adam. Another outstanding feature of Moccas is the beautiful flying staircase, built under an oval dome. Although the house is in private ownership, the gardens and ground floor are open one day a week throughout the summer.

Dinmore Manor
Manor —
14th-century
piscina

The Commandery of the Knights Hospitaller of St John of Jerusalem, their manor-house and chapel, are set in a thousand acres of fields and woodland at the top of Dinmore Hill, looking out towards the Malverns. Here is a basically 17th-century house with modern reconstructions in the medieval style. The grassy lawn, however, covers a cobbled yard which flanks the oldest part of the site, the Hospitallers' chapel. Of the chapel's 12th-century walls only a buttress stands, but the rest of the 14th-century chapel with its fine timber ceiling is in good condition. The hinges and strap-work on the chapel's doors are very ancient.

The chapel and the Knights' Commandery were endowed at some time between 1163 and 1188 by Thomas de Dunamore. The list of his successors, down to 1540, is recorded on the chapel wall. Many 15th-century documents survive which record the inviolable sanctuary of Dinmore, but none of their domestic buildings has survived. It is believed that many members of the order are buried here.

The earliest part of the nearby manor-house was built in the late 16th century but there are traces of 12th-century foundations, walls and woodwork within the house. Interesting additions were made to the house in the 1930s by the owner Richard Hollins Murray, inventor of 'cats-eyes'. The entrance to Dinmore from the main road is indicated by a signpost picked out in these 'Murray-signs' as they should properly be named.

Dinmore
Manor —
tower

His additions, in Pre-Raphaelite style, include a lofty music-room with a fine hammer-beam roof and, uncharacteristic for the Hospitallers, a cloister. The honest guide-book makes it clear that these additions have no real historical significance in the Commandery's ancient history, but they are, somehow, happily placed here. Even the eight circular windows, brightly glazed in modern stained glass by Morris of Westminster, with the new stonework

71

*Eastnor
Castle —
detail*

carefully crafted by local workmen especially trained for the work, blend sensibly in a well-kept water garden to make an affectionate setting for the house and a memorable modern memorial to the Knights of St John. Part of the house and its garden, kept in private ownership, are hospitably open all the year round.

On yet another site, said to be that of the last stand of Caractacus after the storming of the neighbouring British hill-fort by the Romans, is the modern castle of Eastnor, built by the first Lord Somers. Under its foundation stone he buried a coin of the reign of Queen Elizabeth I, in whose time his family first came to Eastnor, and a 3s. bank token of 1811, the year his building was begun. Eastnor Castle's plan is that of a central keep, with massive turrets at the four corners. Lord Somers achieved his aspiration to a home in the style of the great medieval castle, a fortress strong enough to withstand the attacks of long ago, if not today's. The architect was Sir Robert Smirke RA, who chose to use local stone and timber for the building. Trees came into short supply owing to the demands of the navy for ships to defend England against Napoleon. Sir Robert therefore introduced iron stanchions to replace traditional wooden roof-trusses. The death of his heir in the Peninsular War understandably dampened Lord Somers' enthusiasm for the building and it was left to the second and third earls to finish Eastnor Castle.

Today the lofty Great Hall, designed by George Gilbert Scott, is crowded with a large collection of armour, representing several centuries and many lands. This gives the Hall a museum-like atmosphere which is dispelled on entering the dining room. This family room contains portraits by Van Dyck, Lely and Kneller, and is overhung by a beautiful rock crystal chandelier. The Gothic drawing-room, designed by Pugin, is an outstanding example of Victorian flamboyance. The 63-foot library is hung with tapestries woven in 1620 by Flemish weavers in Paris. The room contains more than 5,000 books. The room with the greatest charm is undoubtedly the Octagon Saloon, with its specially made Indian carpet and yet another outstanding chandelier. One of the room's most interesting pieces of furniture is a fine 18th-century Dutch longcase clock, with moving figures. The castle is now owned by the sixth earl's daughter, who welcomes visitors during the summer months. The grounds are no longer kept in the style of early 19th-century pleasure-gardens, but have many of the original trees.

These and many other country houses in Herefordshire well illustrate the county's fortunes and commemorate the notable families who lived in them.

XIV The Civil War in Herefordshire

Herefordshire was by tradition a thoroughly royalist county, yet there was an unusual absence of resident royalist nobility in the county. The only truly local peer was Viscount Scudamore of Holme Lacy. Preoccupied with his library and orchards, he was no 'malignant' cavalier. Others of the county's landed aristocracy were the earl of Essex, later named by parliament as the county's lord lieutenant, and the dowager countess of Kent, both absentee landlords. The most influential class were the gentry, a group of moderate families like the Kyrles of Walford and Marcle, the Hoptons of Canon Frome, the Vaughans, Skipps and Coningsbys. There were no well-defined 'middle classes' of wealthy, non-landed townsmen; even in the market towns the gentry were dominant. Herefordshire's squirearchy were conservative in their politics, even a few ageing supporters of parliament's cause, like Sir Richard Hopton of Canon Frome, father of a cavalier, or Sir John Kyrle of Much Marcle, who would change sides three times. An educated minority, advocating the Presbyterian cause, was headed by Robert Harley at Brampton Bryan, but this was scarcely an 'opposition' to Charles I's personal rule. Faced with regicide and republicanism, these men too would prove to be moderate.

From 1630 to 1640, Charles antagonised his most loyal supporters as well as his critics by a period of autocratic rule without parliament. To finance this, he revived archaic sources of medieval and Tudor taxation, such as levies of 'coat and conduct money' for the militia, and profitable trading monopolies – the Coningsbys did well out of soap. Long-lost forest dues were once more collected, and, above all, Ship Money was levied on inland counties. Ship Money was the issue which most tended to erode the loyalty of Herefordshire's gentry, who were set the invidious task of acting as unpaid collectors of an unpopular tax. The county was assessed in 1635 for a quota of £4,000, the boroughs of Leominster and Hereford paying contributions within that sum of £100 (Leominster) and £250 (Hereford).

The county pleaded poverty in a petition from its landed gentry. The 1630s had been marred by widespread pestilence and failure of harvests. Cattle prices were low, and sheep-farmers felt the pressure of foreign competition. A visitation of plague in 1637 had reduced the town of Ross to poverty, and decimated the parishes of Yatton,

Walford and Bridstow. As a result, the first demand was reduced to £3,500 and fell as low as £1,200 in 1638. At parish level, the collectors were the village constables; over them, the sheriffs exercised an uneasy lack of control. Threats by the Privy Council dismissed the sheriff's excuses 'at their peril' as the tax remained unpaid. Sheriff John Alderne, 'weary of imprisoning constables', found these to be no idle threats when he was himself imprisoned for the county's default. Passive resistance proved more effective than protest. Year by year, the cumulative arrears remained unpaid. The county's quotas for 1635 and 1636 were 98 per cent paid within five years, but in 1641, 45 per cent of the 1638 quota, and 81 per cent of that for 1639, were still outstanding. In 1640, the mayor of Hereford refused to hand over collected tax until there was a decision on the legality of Ship Money. One of the first acts of the Long Parliament in 1640 was to abolish the tax.

The gate of Brampton Bryan Castle

Another heartfelt Presentment by the county's Grand Jury in 1640 paid more attention to economic grievances than to political opposition. The gentry appealed to Magna Carta against illegal weirs along the Wye which stopped water-borne trade, 'especially a prejudice to the Citty of Hereford'. They deplored the importation of Spanish wool which competed with the county's staple product 'to the great damadge of the whole Countie' and opposed the working of iron mills, some standing within five miles of the city, which had caused great destruction of timber trees and a rise in fuel prices. Only incidentally did the Jury complain of political grievances. They challenged the traditional jurisdiction of the prerogative Court of Wales and the Marches based on Ludlow. Herefordshire, they said, was 'an ancient Englishe county and no part of Wales, nor the Marches of the same'. It is significant that the gentry who signed this protest included as many future royalists as parliament men. Together, they include Wallop Brabazon of Leominster, Croft of Croft Castle, Lingen of Sutton, Rudhall of Ross, Vaughan of Moccas, with Hopton, Kyrle and Scudamore of Kentchurch. On some issues, Herefordshire gentry were united.

In 1640, however, when faced by war with Scotland, Charles was forced to summon a parliament, Herefordshire's elections divided the members almost exactly between royalists and roundheads. The county chose Fitzwilliam Coningsby of Hampton Court, a cavalier, and Robert Harley. Hereford city elected Richard Seaborne, later disabled and imprisoned on the capture of the city in 1645, and Richard Weaver, businessman, magistrate and parliamentarian. 'Lempster' chose two lawyers, Samson Eure of Gatley Park who became Speaker of the king's Oxford parliament, and Walter Kyrle of

74

Walford, father of The Man of Ross, a vacillating member of the 'popular' party. Only Weobley was solidly royalist, returning Arthur Jones and Thomas Tomkyns. By 1652, none of these M.P.s still kept their seats. Those who had not joined the king, been imprisoned or sequestered as royalists, had been 'purged' by their own leaders for too-moderate views.

Before 1642, the attitude of most Herefordshire folk to rumours of national unrest can best be described as moderate conservatism, a traditional loyalty to crown and church, rather than active support of either side. Even religious dissension was defused by the uncontroversial attitude of Bishop George Coke (1636-46), a moderate churchman who was no doctrinaire follower of the unpopular Archbishop Laud.

In Herefordshire, the most vigorous defender of parliament's cause was Lady Brilliana Harley of Brampton Bryan, Sir Robert's third, younger wife. Born in 1600, she was daughter of the governor of the Brill in Holland, from which her name derived. A surviving collection of Lady Harley's letters describes family life at Brampton as war began. She regrets the changing relationships with her neighbours, brought about by their religious and political differences. In a letter to her son Edward, who had been a favourite of Sir William Croft of Croft Castle, she wrote 'Sir William gave me a slight visit ... he never asked how your father did'. Sir William was active in raising forces for the king. Other neighbours, once her friends, were also pledged to the royalist cause.

By 1643, her awareness of increasing isolation becomes evident. The safety of family and tenants now depended on her alone, with her husband and son away. Servants brought back tales of having been reviled as 'Roundheads' in the streets of Hereford, and she dreaded the drunken violence of Leintwardine's fair-day. In 1642, she heard threats of the militia's mustering. She derived little comfort from the chivalrous marquis of Hertford, royalist commander in Hereford, who assured her that she need not fear him, but must beware of his successor, Lord Herbert.

In 1643, a royalist council of war decided to destroy Brampton Castle. Sir William Vavasour, governor of Hereford, in a letter to Prince Rupert, emphasised that 'I had been lost in the opinion of these counties, neither should I get half the contributions promised me, unless I make an attempt upon Sir Robert Harley's house'. Vavasour did not, however, offer force immediately. He invited Lady Brilliana to surrender, meeting her to parley within the castle walls. She was not persuaded, and the cavaliers brought up a force of 600 men. The castle's garrison was composed of 100 armed men, two 'drakes' or small cannon mounted on the walls, and two months' supply of powder. Reinforcements turned out to be a meagre musket, a bandolier or two and, more effectively, the services of a veteran sergeant. On 27 July, Lord Molyneaux led several troops of horse with foot and cannon to take position. This formidable array failed to shake Brilliana's resolution. When a blind man was murdered outside her gates, she was strengthened in her righteous cause. The 'malignant' forces were commanded by Colonel Lingen, and the siege lasted seven weeks. The castle's cook was shot by a poisoned bullet, 'which murdered him in great torment', and a running spring which furnished the town was poisoned at the fountain. The Harley estate suffered heavy losses and Brampton village was reduced to ruins. Nearby, Wigmore castle was destroyed.

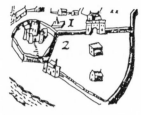

Hereford Castle as it appears on Speed's map of the city

Throughout the siege, Brilliana was torn by anxieties about her son Edward, now a colonel of parliamentary horse, and fear of surrender. Her letters, often written on hidden pieces of cloth, were in elaborate code. 'I acknowledge the great mercy of God that He preserved you in so sharp a fight when your horse was killed ... I thank God my provision has held out'. She lacked guidance from Sir Robert. 'I desire your father would seriously think what I had best do, whether stay at Brampton or remove to some other place'.

In her last letter of 9 October 1643, Brilliana's faith in God was as strong as ever. She wrote to 'Colonell' Edward Harley: 'I am now again threatened ... but I hope the Lord will deliver me. I have taken a very great cold, which has made me very ill these two or three days, but I hope the Lord will be merciful to me, in giving me my health, for it is an ill time to be sick in ...'. Her adversaries dispersed, but for Lady Brilliana it was too late. Her 'great cold' proved too much for her, and a few days later she died, leaving the keeping of the castle to her faithful friend Dr. Nathaniel Wright. A year later Brampton surrendered to Sir Michael Woodhouse.

For the most part, the county experienced a quiet war, as the rival armies marched past to Chester, Gloucester, Worcester or Wales. Herefordshire's chief importance to the king's cause was as a source of provisions, horses and pressed men for service elsewhere. There was no pitched battle of the Civil War in Herefordshire. Massey's parliamentary force in the west was based on Gloucester, so that military activity tended to manoeuvre around Ross and Ledbury, rather than advancing towards the centre of the county.

Hereford city experienced a peaceful royalist occupation until 1645, a relatively uneventful parliamentary occupation thereafter. Two premature parliamentary victories were achieved unopposed, firstly by the earl of Stamford for Essex in 1642, and again by Waller in 1643.

76

Both generals, after brief, unpopular sojourns, left the city to its own devices. Hereford staunchly withstood investment by Cromwell's Scottish soldiers in 1645, but fell victim to a surprise attack by Colonels Morgan and Birch moving in from Ledbury in 1646. Leominster gave in more readily, and was well-advised to do so, for a short burst of musketry fire in Hereford's Commercial Street, as Birch's foresters stormed in through Bister Gate at dawn, rendered the city technically open to capture by assault rather than surrender. This legitimised plundering by the victorious roundheads.

The occupation of the city is vividly described by Joyce Jefferies, a Hereford citizen whose companions were 'a cat and a throstle in a twiggen cage'. Her journals and account books cover the years 1638 to 1647. They show Mrs. Jefferies to be a woman of sound financial standing. Her income of £800 a year (£120,000 today) was derived partly from an annuity from her half-brother Humphrey Coningsby, and from interest on money lent to her neighbours. Such influential clients gave Joyce Jefferies social status. Nor did she deny herself. Her love of fine clothes is shown by her purchase of 'a black silk Calimancoe gowne, petticoat and bodice'. The bill, including the making, came to £18 1s 8d (perhaps £2,700 today).

In 1640 the king raised an army to fight the Scots. Mrs. Jefferies gave money to those about to enlist. She paid Miles Hacklint 2s 6d and her cousin William Coningsby 1s. She records:

> This day the trained soldiers went towards Scotland. I gave John Lincoln, that went with Captain Button, 6d., and three soldiers of the same company, for drink, 4d.

When in 1642 king and parliament quarrelled over raising the militia, she came upon soldiers discharging their muskets near her house. Undaunted, on 18 May she 'gave the soldier who shot off at my window, 1s and beer'. When the news reached her that the earl of Essex had left London on a journey north, Mrs. Jefferies rallied to the royalist cause. She paid 20s to a Hereford mercer for weapons and artillery to strengthen the city, and on 20 September paid her own soldier 10s for seven days' training with Captain Richard Wigmore. On the 25th, news reached Hereford that Essex had entered Worcester. Mrs. Jefferies took flight to her cousin's house at Kilmington, taking as many of her 'beds and boxes' as she could carry.

Hereford was entered by a parliamentary regiment of foot and some horse-troopers on 30 September. They confiscated royalist property. Mrs. Jefferies recorded how on 4 October, 'Captain Hammond and his barbarous company' plundered her house. 'They took away my two bay coach mares, much linen and Eliza Acton's clothes [her godchild]'. She took steps to recover what she could, paying one Matthias Rufford 21s 6d to redeem 'from Captain Hammond's soldiers, my two black beaver hats and two gold bands, out of the thieves' and plunderers' hands'. In April 1644, she planned to move into a new town-house, but in 1645 Colonel Scudamore, preparing for another siege, ordered many orchards and houses to be levelled for defence, including Mrs. Jefferies' property. She noted a payment of 18d for removing the window-glass and burying it in chests in the garden. The following year she paid a further 6d to the bailiff of Horncastle for digging the chests up again.

Goodrich Castle

The Parliamentarian committee tried to confiscate her property, but Mrs. Jefferies bore this calamity with fortitude and generosity. On 24 March 1647 she gave 'a shilling to a poor minister, John Powell, and his wife, who were going to London to beg relief, having been plundered by Sir Michael Woodhouse and his soldiers of all they had'. Her journal ends in 1650, but Joyce Jefferies lived for another three years. She is buried in the chancel of the parish church of Clifton-upon-Teme.

After the capture of Charles I in 1646, Herefordshire was borne on a political tide which swept the country from moderate parliamentary victory to a military junta which divided parliamentarians. Dissension began between moderate Presbyterians like Harley and a more militant, Independent, army. This conflict is illustrated by the Harleys' quarrel with the roundhead Colonel Birch, though their differences were as much a matter of personal jealousy as of political conflict. Both Harley and Birch lost their seats in Pride's purge of the Commons in 1648; the Harleys lost their influence in the county too. Regicide and an Oath of Engagement to a republic made the political situation increasingly unacceptable to moderate men.

The royalist cause was staunchly maintained by Sir Harry Lingen of Sutton St Michael. Born in 1612, at the age of 26 he followed family tradition as sheriff of Herefordshire. Cut off in Hereford when it was captured in 1646, Lingen escaped across the frozen Wye with Sir Barnaby Scudamore, and continued to resist the parliamentary occupation at the vacant castle of Goodrich, which he fortified and defended with 200 men. Because his party consisted of 'mostly cavaliers, bold men, knowing every ford and bridleway through the district', they were able to constantly harass the king's enemies in the county. Undaunted by Birch's attack on the stables at Goodrich, Lingen saw the governor's absence as a chance to capture Hereford. He led 30 troopers to its gates and in broad daylight slew the sentries, 'cut the turnpike', and forced his way into the city. Lack of support from the townsfolk and the mustering of the garrison caused Lingen to retreat, but he evaded pursuit.

A further attack was mounted on Goodrich, over which the king's standard still flew. The defenders were promised 'civility', but Lingen, well aware that the captured king had relinquished all strongholds, would accept none but a royal order to surrender. The castle's water-supply was cut off, mines were dug, and the largest mortar in England, 'Roaring Meg', was brought to bear on the keep. (The cannon now stands in Churchill Gardens in Hereford.) Goodrich's roof was destroyed, the walls breached. Further resistance was impossible, and on 31 July after six weeks' siege Goodrich surrendered and the defenders' lives were spared. They marched out boldly to a traditional country air, afterwards known as 'Harry Lingen's fancy'. Less than a week after his release, Lingen reappeared in Hereford 'with his sword on his thigh', but was unmolested.

Lingen remained a popular figure. He allayed suspicion by taking the Covenant, which bound him over not to bear arms. This did not prevent him from receiving a commission from the Prince of Wales in 1648, when royalist fortunes seemed about to turn. Lingen planned a rising 'by divers knights, colonels, gentlemen and others' for the king, to associate the four counties of Staffordshire, Worcestershire, Herefordshire, and Shropshire ... restore his Majesty's glory and honour'. The rising failed, and soon Lingen was a prisoner himself, and no more is heard of him until the Restoration, when he was elected as Hereford's M.P. He died in 1662 and is buried at Stoke Edith.

During the Commonwealth Herefordshire was ruled by an elaborate system of committees. Regionally, the county belonged to an Association based on Gloucester, which included Gloucestershire, Herefordshire, Monmouthshire and South Wales. Nearer home, Herefordshire was ruled by the county committee. A sequestration committee organised the confiscation and income from royalist estates, especially the lands of bishop, dean and chapter, which had been sold off or leased. This committee paid poor relief and levied regular fines on royalist sympathisers. The militia committee mustered local forces, which the Harleys endeavoured to use to restore their waning local influence. An assessment committee raised regular monthly taxes on royalists and republicans alike; these funds were essential to maintain a standing 'schismatical' army. Occasionally, local government was overridden by visitations from major-generals or sequestration commissioners from London.

As to the Anglican church in Herefordshire, only 49 of the 200 parish and cathedral clergy were ejected to be replaced by

Independent preachers. Some, like Andrew Adney, vicar of Canon Frome, were accused of being 'very scandalous in life and conversation and unfit for the ministry'. John Powell of Wacton was said to be 'a common frequenter of alehouses, a swearer much suspected of incontinency'. To such accusations the county committee often added the more dangerous charge: 'also active and incendious against Parliament'. This was the reason given for the ejection of Roger Breinton, rector of Staunton-on-Wye and Credenhill. Three of the bishop's sons were deprived of their livings. Their father was captured at Hereford in 1645, imprisoned in Gloucester, and his episcopal estates were forfeited to parliament. Coke was then taken to London, where he died within the year, the see remaining vacant until the Restoration.

Others followed a more militant path. Informers reported of Prebendary William Sherborne that during 1650 he resided in royalist Oxford, riding armed with sword and pistols on secret intelligence missions for the king. James Reade, rector of Mansell Gamage and Byford, was so active during the siege of Hereford in 1645 that King Charles gave him a golden ring as a keepsake.

Nowhere was the tragedy of intolerance more brutally demonstrated than at Tarrington in 1644. There the vicar, a 'reverend man of above four-score', was apprehended by a troop of Massey's horse, who rudely asked him who he was for. The old gentleman answered '"For God and the King" ... for which the barbarous rebel shot him through the head with his Pistoll'. Others had less to lose. John Clark, vicar of Norton Canon, held a living too small to be worth sequestrating. He was molested by the local people, and 'robbed of his hat on a wet day, being forced to wear his maid's'.

Many other clergymen weathered the storm. The ejected vicar of Ashperton, 'with other confederate clergy and malignant gentry', opened an alehouse in Worcester. Others were permitted to become village schoolmasters or tutors in private houses. A few old men survived to be reinstated at the Restoration. John Coke, the bishop's son, was restored to Whitbourne in 1660 and lived on for nearly twenty years. Longest-lived of all was William Hosier, vicar of Blakemere, who died aged 100 as Keeper of the Vicar's College in 1708 – 60 years after the king's execution.

During the occupation, there were only a few abortive attempts to restore the royalist cause in Herefordshire. On one dramatic occasion, a committee member, Silas Taylor, was accused of permitting a royalist meeting to take place under cover of a musical concert. Little was done, however, to rally to Charles II during his nearby Worcester campaign in 1651. Not until the Restoration did royalist families like

28. Elizabeth Barrett Browning (1806–1861) from a posthumous bust of 1864, by William Wetmore Story. Her letters and diaries describe her early life at Hope End, near Ledbury.

29. Brilliana, Lady Harley (1600–1643), whose steadfast defence of her husband's castle at Brampton Bryan against a Royalist force is recorded in letters to her husband Sir Robert and her son Colonel Edward Harley.

30.   The bearded figure of Rev. Francis Kilvert, Vicar of Bredwardine from 1877 to 1879, belies his relative youth. Married only five weeks, he died of peritonitis aged 39 years.

31. Built in 1621, the Old House is a famous landmark of Hereford. Originally part of a row of houses known as Butchery Row, it now stands in isolation as a museum on the High Town pedestrian precinct. Several rooms are furnished in 17th-century style.

32. The kitchen of the Old House contains the typical 17th-century domestic furniture, 'treen' ware and pewter, described in Herefordshire probate inventories.

33. Homme House, in Much Marcle, where Kilvert was a wedding-guest in 1874. 'After the wedding breakfast, we were all photographed on the steps before the house'.

34. The *Red Lion* coaching inn at Leominster, now an antique shop, off-licence and District Planning office.

35. The Market House, Ledbury.

the Brabazons, Vaughans, Cornewalls, and Lingens regain their former influence in the county. Many others, like the Kyrles, the Scudamores and the Hoskins, had survived the political storms. An increasing number of local figures were new men from the towns, the neighbouring counties or further afield. The man who most blatantly personified the changing fortunes of political intrigue was not a native of Herefordshire. This was Colonel John Birch, whose monument dominates the chancel of Weobley church. A Lancastrian by birth, with no formal education, he had a long-lasting sense of inferiority which drove him to achieve success. Whilst still a packhorse carrier in the West Country, his military talent became apparent to Cromwell in the defence of Bristol against Prince Rupert. He was appointed successively Governor of Bridgwater, Bath and Bristol.

In 1646, instructed to take Hereford, he was warned that 'the city will be more difficult to keep than to capture'. Birch took the city by surprise, using information obtained from bribed royalist deserters, and stormed Bister Gate at dawn. Appointed governor of Hereford, he found the prediction came true. Commandeering the bishop's palace as his residence, he failed to gain the citizens' respect. His uneasy rule ended in martial law.

Birch now turned to politics. Rejected by the 'county voices', he found favour with the burgesses of Leominster, whose town he had saved from plundering earlier that year. He was returned as M.P. for Leominster in 1646, 1654 and 1656, but was one of those excluded from taking his seat for his opposition to army rule. He was still influential in Herefordshire, even 'popular in these parts'. He sold Hereford Castle to the Harleys and refortified the bishop's manor-house at Whitbourne, as a retreat in the north of the county. In 1655 he was arrested there and imprisoned in Hereford gaol under suspicion of royalist sympathies.

At the Restoration, Birch was returned to the Cavalier Parliament as M.P. for Penryn in Cornwall. When forfeited lands were restored to the church, he was glad of royal favour in securing leases on some of his Herefordshire estates. He became an active committee-man, described by the regicide Ludlow as 'a nimble gentleman and one who used to neglect no opportunity of providing for himself'. Samuel Pepys makes several references to Birch in his diaries for 1660-8. His first impressions were not favourable: 'Colonel Birch was very impertinent and troublesome'. There is cause for suspicion that some of Birch's dealings were dishonest. In 1668 Pepys records that Birch was, with Roger Vaughan of Moccas and others, 'in trouble about the prize business'.

Birch's ultimate ambition was to become one of the Herefordshire landed gentry. He told Pepys 'of the general want of money in the country, so that land sold for nothing and that many pennyworth he knew of lands and houses upon them with good titles [in Herefordshire]'. During the Commonwealth Birch had invested heavily in church lands in Herefordshire, convinced that the bishops' surrender of their estates would be permanent. His opposition to episcopacy was, unlike Lady Brilliana's, not a matter of religious conviction. He foresaw personal gain in the bishops' downfall. In 1661 Vaughan sold Birch his wife Ann's house, Garnstone near Weobley for £1,500, or £4 an acre. Birch was now the wealthiest landowner in Weobley. Ann's family, the Tomkyns, had been M.P.s for Leominster or Weobley since 1624. Birch was now almost guaranteed a safe alternative to his seat in Cornwall. He became M.P. for Weobley from 1679 until his death in 1691, contesting elections regularly with Thomas Foley of Stoke Edith, as one of Shaftesbury's first Whigs.

Birch dreamed of founding a dynasty, but this was denied him; none of his sons survived. Birch's efforts to impress posterity became ludicrous, as the pantomime of the erection of a republican monument in Weobley's Anglican church demonstrates. Its position, and the arrogant sentiments of the inscription, caused riots in the borough. Traces of the railings which his unfortunate son-in-law erected to protect the memorial can still be seen in the church wall.

For others, whether parliamentarian like the Harleys or royalist like Mrs. Jefferies, the war brought only personal tragedy and financial loss. Birch, although he may have ended his life as something of a local eccentric, had a career which exemplifies both the pickings which the war and its aftermath offered to the ambitious and unscrupulous, and the success of the compromise Restoration settlement, which allowed erstwhile opponents like Birch and Vaughan to sit together in the Commons, planning Herefordshire land deals.

XV Seventeenth-Century Homes

The Herefordshire domestic scene was richly illustrated in the 17th century by hundreds of probate inventories, from a time when proving a will required the preparation of a list of all the deceased's possessions. Inventories list 'all the goods, chattels, cattle and debts' down to the last spoon or 'muck in the yard, lumber and trumpery in the barn'. They record possessions of householders as diverse as a poverty-stricken widow, substantial yeoman or wealthy merchant.

Herefordshire's inventories are not collected in print, but the originals are indexed at the Record Office. The main series begins after 1600 and is very full for the Restoration period. These are diocesan records but 26 parishes are separately collected as the 'peculiar' jurisdiction of the Dean. These provide valuable evidence of tradesmen in the 17th-century city.

An early household, of 1592, is that of Roger Conynge of Tedstone Delamere. The total value of his possessions was £97 11s 8d (about £15,000 today), three-quarters of it being tied up in farming stock. He had six expensive oxen, 15 head of cattle, four calves, a bull, a mare and a colt, with pigs, geese and hens and four 'stalls' of bees. There was corn and hay in the barns worth £20 10s – one-third of all his farm stock. He also owned two cottages, lands and rents in Avenbury. Conynge's house was sparsely furnished with 'beddstids, beds, beddynge and Lynen ware'. He had no chairs or 'joyned' tables, only trestle table-boards, forms and stools. His utensils were of brass, pewter and iron, the only luxury four small silver spoons worth 10s. His least investment was his 'wearing apparell', valued at only 10s, less than one per cent of his possessions. (Other Herefordshire inventories record two to ten per cent of the inventories' value as clothing.) Nearly a quarter of his wealth was in money lent to 14 debtors, in sums ranging from six shillings to £3 each. Moneylending is regularly recorded in inventories at this time when banks were unknown. Conynge left almost all his possessions to 'my bastard daughter, Sybill Conynge'. He adds the conventional 'dole' of a penny to be paid to the poor of the parish on the day of his funeral.

For an ordinary villager, Roger Conynge was unusually rich; other inventories record pitifully small lists of possessions. The meagre home of Widow Sayce in 1666 is typical. The two rooms of her cottage in Bullinghope were an open hall and 'the further room of my

Quatrefoil window: Weobley

83

dwelling-house'. Her chattels amounted to only £8 5s 2d. She had a cow, a sow, four little pigs and some corn in the barn. Like Conynge's, this small farm stock is the major portion of her estate. The household furniture again is the basic requirement of one person. Her tiny hall is panelled, like many a living room in the city's Forestreet, for it has a 'wainscott cubbord'. Joan had a little brass pan, one pot, a chafing-dish and a pail, but there is no mention of knives or spoons; she lighted her house with one brass candlestick. The bedchamber had a corded bedstead, with feather-bed, pillow and 'coverlid', with two pairs of sheets kept in a coffer. She left the brass pot and two pewter dishes to her son Francis and 'all the rest of my worldly goods to my daughter, Mary Sayce'. There was in the end not much to bequeath. There is a laconic entry at the end of the inventory:

Total: £8 5s 2d
Debts to be paid: £3 0s 0d
Funeral expenses: £2 10s 0d
Balance: £2 15s 2d

The record office's card-index identifies occupations, from barber-surgeons to yeomen. Apart from husbandmen, the largest class named, the most numerous craftsmen are weavers, especially at Bosbury, Ledbury, Walford, Aymestrey, Kington, Ross and Weobley. There were tanners at Leominster, Kinnersley, Ross and Brampton Abbots, glovers in Hereford, Ross, Leominster, Pixley, Lyonshall and Pembridge. Another widespread trade is that of the mercers or shopkeepers: unfortunately, the goods in their shops and their working tools are rarely listed. An exception to this general rule is the splendid inventory of John Jones, a mercer of Hereford, which was edited by F.C. Morgan and published in the *Transactions of the Woolhope Club* for 1942. This lists hundreds of yards of cloth – 'buckram, callicoe, lynnen, Indean silk and tafity' – as well as buttons, thimbles, children's caps and muffs, shoelaces, and ribbons.

The inventory of Philip Price, a glover of Aylestone Hill in Hereford, is also unusually full. Price had five feather-beds with blankets and coverlets, also, as is often the case with 17th-century folk, a great deal of linen. He had 28 pairs of sheets and 42 table napkins, fine and coarse. His pots and pans are made of brass, with two dozen pieces of pewter and a touch of luxury in a Kidderminster carpet and three cushions. As well as his gloving trade, Price kept a substantial smallholding, with pigs and sheep, a heifer, mare and colt, and some poultry. There was eight pounds' worth of corn in his barn, and 12 loads of hay. The total value of his estate, including leases of arable land in Aylestone's field and £115 in debts, half of them 'desparate', is £228. He had three hogsheads of beer and household provisions worth three pounds. The largest proportion of his wealth was invested in his stock of gloves and sheepskins:

5 dozen of Cordovan gloves, rough, worth: £3 15s
25 doz. double-sewn sheep-leather gloves, rough: £15 0s
60 doz. in-seam leather gloves, cut but unmade: £18 0s
22 doz. sheep-leather gloves, cut but unmade: 12s
I cwt and 8 lbs of wool: £2 0s
In the lime-pit, 2 doz. sheepskin pelts: 5s

Most village inventories list household goods without reference to different rooms, but a few give some indications of the plan of a 17th-century house. The main room was the hall, with its open fire. Other rooms might be built overhead, as in 'the chamber over the parlour'. Richard Fox, a wealthy wheelwright in 1645, had an eight-roomed house of two storeys at Brimfield. On the ground floor were a hall, a parlour, a middle room used for brewing, a buttery with three barrels of beer, a kitchen and three upstairs rooms.

Town houses had even more rooms. In 1600 Philip Aston had a 12-roomed house in Hereford, built over a cellar. There was a wainscoted hall with adjoining buttery, parlour and two kitchens. Upstairs were the Green, Yellow and White Chambers, the Rush Chamber, and a room over the hall. One bedroom had a fireplace, and there were two or three beds in each room. Some were trundle beds for servants, stored under the larger beds when not in use. At the stairhead was a great chest and a little desk. Kept in the buttery for the five bedrooms were five each of flagons, pewter candlesticks and chamber-pots, as well as 12 pairs of sheets, 36 table-napkins and a tablecloth.

At the house of John Wolfe, a Hereford baker, in 1661, there was a 'chamber over the shop', a chimney-chamber with an old carpet, a standing bedstead, coffer and chair, and a 'dark back room, next to the garden'. The 'keeling' or cooling-room was the dairy, which dairy had vats with straw covers and three stone troughs, also feather-beds and green flannel curtains on rods.

One of the more elaborate city inventories is that of Mary Williams, taken in 1663. Her house was large and well-appointed, and the rooms had imposing names, reminiscent of an inn or official residence. There were, apart from the cellar and buttery, a Bell Chamber, Sun Chamber, King's Head Chamber, The Lyon and Rose Chambers, Crown Chamber and 'Dollsine'. These were bed-sitting rooms, all upholstered in green. Only the Dollsine breaks the overall colour-scheme with a yellow rug and blue bed-curtains. This was evidently

Great wheel

85

an important 'public' house, with two dozen joined stools in the Rose Room and 84 table-napkins, some, like the 16 pairs of sheets, of Welsh yarn. The kitchen had a large assortment of pots, tools and utensils, such as flesh-forks, mincing-knife, gridiron and iron dripping-pan. There was a jack-chain, with three spits, and various vessels of brass or 'latting'. The cellar was full of red and white wines, sherry, Canary and Malaga, about three hundred gallons in all. The total value of Mrs. Williams' goods was £212, including clothes valued at £10 and £145 worth of 'good debts'.

Craftsmen's inventories rarely itemise their tools. John Lloyd, a clothmaker, had an apprentice's chamber and kept a 'shoppe' containing a settle, three pairs of shears, 'the working tools belonging to ther trade of a walker' (i.e. a fuller) and 'a parcel of old garlick'. Once again, for four bedsteads there are four chamber-pots, kept in the kitchen with four pewter candlesticks. John Finch, a bellfounder, has in his shop only his tools, but in the Bell-House we find 'one beam with scales, one set of pulleys, a hammer and two ladders'. All this is worth only 18s, out of an inventory totalling £19 13s 4d. Bartholomew Taylor's chandler's house in 1665 had a hall, buttery and parlour, with a shop containing a flaxwheel, a small parcel of wick-yarn, and one and a half pounds of candles. In the 'work-house' was a candle-mould, 'an old kettle fixed to the house in the nature of a furnace', one brazier with an iron beam, 'a screw to screw tallow', some candle-staves and 'other pitiful old trumpery'. All this working stock is worth barely one pound; Bartholomew was evidently only in a small way of business.

Leather chair

It is rare indeed to find a person's garments listed in detail, but the will of John Forde, a mercer of Leominster, paints a colourful picture of Jacobean costume reminiscent of Malvolio himself. In 1623 Forde made a remarkable will, listing small gifts of ribbons, garters, and gloves. His major bequest was to John Hyggins of Winslow, who received: 'one black hatt with a ribband about it, one double band and white flannel waistcote, one green fustian doublet, one grey friese jerkin, one pair of green hose with buttons down the side, one pair of white woolen stockings and one pair of sadd, cruel [i.e. drab, tight] garters'. John also left a contribution to his father's wardrobe: 'My best Hatt and hat-band, my best cloak, my best hose, doublet and jerkin, one pair of worsted stockings, tawny coloured and one pair of lynnen stockings'. That is how a Leominster shopkeeper dressed in 1623!

To compare the values of all these goods with present-day prices is a fallible exercise with too many variable factors. Mary Williams' cellar-full of wine, for example, averages five pence a gallon, compared with, say, £24 today. Here a comparison already fraught by differences in measurement, quality, coinage and price is further skewed by modern excise duty. We can compare average prices of cattle, acres of corn on the ground, bushels of malt, beer at one and a half old pence a gallon and 60 yards of flannel, then valued at two and a half old pence, now four pounds the yard. If we can find enough stable items, preferably exact quantities of silver, and make comparable inventories of 20 to 30 identical items, we find that the present cost of the same goods is on average 150 times in 1984 than in 1660. This makes too little allowance for seasonal and local variations, and probably rates the accuracy of the original 'praysors' too high. Furniture values too are almost impossible to compare. Can we think of Mary Williams's turned chairs as equivalent to 'any modern chair'? If we do not consider quality or age, then each of Roger Conynge's small silver spoons is worth £20 by today's average price. If we take their antique value into account, any one of them might be worth as much as £5,000 a spoon. More important than this matching of prices, however, are the differences in the quality of life and home which so many inventories reveal. Each document is a small textbook of social history.

Dragon beam — the Red Lion, *Weobley*

XVI Residents and Travellers

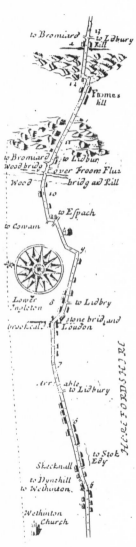

*Extract from Road
Atlas of John
Ogilby, 1765*

As early as 1125, William of Malmesbury, on a visit to Hereford, observed: 'Not large, but still such as to show itself by ruins and broken ditches, to have been something great'. A nostalgic viewpoint is a constant feature of many writers' feelings for this ancient shire.

John Leland, describing his *Itinerary* through Herefordshire and Wales during the 16th century, painted a lively picture. He described the ruined castles of Weobley and Kilpeck, Roman remains at Kenchester, the market towns of Leominster, Pembridge and Ross, and many religious houses. He was impressed by the size of Hereford's castle, which he compared favourably with Windsor. This was 'one of the fairest, largest and strongest castles of England', though now 'it tendithe toward ruin'. The walls and gates of the city 'be right well maintained by the burgesses of the town'. Leland listed the bishop's palaces, in decay at Ross and Ledbury, and noted that 'Erchenfeld is full of enclosures, very full of corne and wood'.

The *Itinerary* gives details of the state of bridges, or lack of them, on the Wye from Hereford to Builth and upriver. Leland lists seven stone bridges on the Lugg below Leominster, including Ford, Hampton, Wistetone, Lugwardine and Mordiford, and those above the town at Kingsland and Limebrook. At Wellington there was a bridge of three stone arches over Wormsley water; elsewhere ancient bridges were repaired with timber.

Sixteenth-century description of Herefordshire is taken up by William Camden, whose *Britannia* was published in 1586. This survey refers not only to ancient books and documents, but to the traveller's evidence. In the cathedral he saw 'but few monuments, save those of the bishops'. Camden says little of the city, which he heard pronounced as 'Hariford', except to mention that the castle 'is now falling into ruin, by age'. He was, however, impressed by 'the beautiful church ... neat college and fair prebendal houses'. He praised the county's rich produce, from noble red-streaked apples to excellent flax, and 'the county's chief glory at present ... the wool caled *Lemster Ore*, which Europe in general prefers to all, except that of Apulia and Tarenton'.

Leominster impressed Camden. The town 'produces so much wheat and excellent white bread that *Lemster bread* and *Weobley ale* are become proverbial ... These advantages of Lemster and the good

88

market they occasion, raised the envy of Hereford and Worcester so much that they procured the king's authority to change the market day'. Camden's history runs with the rivers. He was well aware of the scenic beauty and economic importance of the major river-valleys which had moulded the county's settlements. He described how the Dore 'divides the valley called by the Welch, from the river *Diffrin Dwr*, but by the English *The Golden Vale*, which name it deserves, from its golden, rich and pleasant plenty. The surrounding hills are covered with woods, below which there are corn fields, below these fair and fruitful meadows, and in the middle glides a clear river, on which Robert, lord of Ewias, built a monastery'.

In 1642 Nehemiah Wharton, a roundhead sergeant of Colonel Holles' redcoat regiment, wrote a vivid description of Hereford. He found it 'environed with a strong wall, better than I have seen before, with five gates and a strong bridge of six arches over the river, surpassing Worcester. In the city, there is the stateliest market-place in the kingdom, built with columns, after the manner of the Exchange. The Minster in every way exceeds that of Worcester, but the city in circuit is not as large'. Wharton was less impressed with Hereford's citizens: 'The inhabitants are totally ignorant in the ways of God, and much addicted to drunkenness and other vice, but principally in swearing, so that the children that have scarcely learned to speak, do universally swear stoutly. Many here speak Welsh'.

A generation later, Celia Fiennes was writing her journal of visits from London into Herefordshire. In 1696 she described a visit to the Foley's new house at Stoke Edith, which 'will be very fine when it is completed; there is to be three flat fronts to the garden sides, the right wing of the house is several apartments for the family, two drawing-rooms and the bed-chambers and closets opening both on a terrace of freestone paving at each end'. Hereford she found 'a pretty little town of timber buildings, the streets well pitched and handsome as to length and breadth'. Crossing the Teme into Whitbourne, the road to Stretton Grandison was treacherous after heavy rain. 'This is the worst way I ever went in Worcester or Herrifordshire – its allways a deep sand and soe in winter and with muck is a bad way ... being soe stoney made it more difficult to travel'.

Eighteenth- and nineteenth-century travellers were well provided with road maps. The English road atlas produced by John Ogilby, 'His Majesty's Cosmographer', in 1765, is particularly informative. These strip maps are semi-pictorial, showing hills, churches, and some buildings in elevation. Small plans of the main towns and villages are also drawn, with special attention to crossroads and bridges. The roadside terrain is usually described, as, for instance, arable, commons, parks, or woodland. Ogilby's route from Hereford to Leicester matches the present A4103 to Worcester via Fromes Hill; his London to Aberystwyth road-map includes the A44 from Bromyard to Leominster. The road from Gloucester to Montgomery follows the A49 from Ross to Hereford and the A4110 runs out of Hereford via King's Pyon and Pembridge. The 18th-century version of the A438 and the A480 from Hereford to Lyonshall and Kington are also clearly recognisable.

A generation too early to benefit from Ogilby's road-maps was one of the most distinguished of the county's literary visitors – Daniel Defoe, author of *Robinson Crusoe*. His *Tour Through England and Wales*, published in 1724, was appreciative of the Herefordshire countryside, if not of Hereford. 'From Ludlow, we took our course due south to Lemster, a large trading town by the River Lug. Leominster has nothing very remarkable about it, but that it is a well-built, well-inhabited town. This town, besides its fine wool, is noted for the best wheat and consequently the finest bread. The people of the county are a diligent and laborious people, chiefly addicted to husbandry. They boast, perhaps not without reason, that they have the finest wool, the best hops and the richest cyder in all Britain. One would hardly expect so pleasant and fruitful a county as this, so near the barren mountains of Wales'. Defoe was less complimentary about the city: 'it is truly an old, mean-built and very dirty city, lying low ...'.

A useful set of road-books is *Paterson's Roads*, published in several editions from 1808 to 1828. Paterson provides not a map but a linear route. This strip format is similar to Ogilby's, but made in words, not pictures. Each road is taken as a complete journey, for example, from Hereford to Cardiff, with a summary of distances from one town to another and the total mileage. He identifies places of interest, stately homes, townships and historic sites along the way. The route is marked by finger-posts, with tiny pictures of turnpike gates and bridges. Matched with the first one-inch edition of the Ordnance Survey maps, Paterson's milestones and the sites of many a turnpike gate can often be found by the roadside. Paterson describes each town in detail. For example in 1808:

Extract from Road Atlas of John Ogilby, 1765

Leominster is seated on the Lugg and is noted for its fine wool. Its trade likewise consists in gloves, leather, hat making etc. Near the church are some remains of its Priory, and on a neighbouring hill are the remains of a palace, now called Comfort Castle.
Ledbury is a well-built town, inhabited chiefly by clothiers, who carry on a great trade.
Hereford is an ancient place, but much decayed. The cathedral is a venerable structure. The chief manufacture of this city is gloves. Before the Conquest,

90

Hereford was the local quarters of the Saxons; as it was afterwards of the English, who were stationed here to keep the Welsh in awe.

The most contentious, and possibly the most self-opinionated of the county's visitors was the political orator, ex-soldier, traveller and journalist, William Cobbett. He viewed the Herefordshire scene with a radical farmer's eye, seeing its countryside in contrast to the 'tax-eating wen' of early urban sprawl. Cobbett paid several visits to Mr. William Palmer's 'beautiful place' at Bollitree Castle in Weston-under-Penyard in the years 1821 to 1826. He particularly admired the wooded hillsides, which he compared favourably with those he had seen in New England.

Cobbett railed against absentee landlords and rectors. Weston, he said, 'is remarkable in having a rector who has constantly resided there for 20 years'. Elsewhere he reported empty parsonage houses in four out of five Herefordshire parishes, with large churches empty of people. His travels in 1826 revealed a state of recession in Herefordshire, with poor crops and low prices. 'Even the wheat was only two-thirds crop, barley and oats really next to nothing. The cattle have been nearly starved in many places. Hay is £6 a ton (last year £3), but wool is half last year's price'. He concludes that 'the winds are less uncertain than this calling of a farmer has now become'.

Ross in 1821 he described as 'an old-fashioned town, but very beautifully situated. If there is very little of finery in the appearance of the inhabitants, there is also little of misery. This is a good plain country town or settlement of tradesmen whose business is that of supplying the cultivators of the soil'. In calmer mood, some of this stormy radical's observations are serene. He was enchanted by the sight of a countrywoman and her children in a donkey cart, intrigued to see for the first time 'a plough going without being held'. Best of all, in September 1826 he painted a lovely picture of autumn crocuses in flower in an orchard at Bollitree: 'one of the prettiest sights in the flower world I ever saw in my life'.

The romantic poet Elizabeth Barrett Browning often had to make her travels in a wheelchair. Her father Edward Moulton Barrett, a successful West Indian merchant, bought Hope End in Colwall in 1809, and the family lived there until 1832. A riding accident when she was 14 brought an active childhood to an end. Elizabeth nevertheless still found pleasure in the Herefordshire countryside. She records in her diary on Thursday 30 June 1831 details of a ride which she was able to take: 'I cantered up the road and up the hill without holding the pommel. I enjoyed riding today, in spite of everything'. These memories influenced her later writing. Barton Court in Colwall, which she knew well, may have been the original of 'Leigh Hall' in *Aurora Leigh*, which she wrote in Italy in 1856. It has also been suggested that a member of the Peyton family may have been the model for 'Romney Leigh'. This was her Herefordshire scene:

Hills, vales, woods, nestled in a silver mist;
Farms, granges, doubled up amongst the hills,
And cattle grazing in the watered vales
And cottage chimneys smoking from the woods.

Elizabeth Barrett Browning died in Florence in 1861. Four years before, her father had been buried with his wife in Ledbury. The church has a curious marble memorial which shows this unforgiving father on his deathbed, with an angel at the head of a flight of steps opening the door to heaven. The Barretts' house did not outlast the century, and is now substantially rebuilt, with only the garden and outbuildings which belonged to Elizabeth's youth.

The diarist Francis Kilvert was a country parson, who lived at Bredwardine from 1877 to 1879. He described Herefordshire scenes which are not unfamiliar today. His Herefordshire homeland lay close along the Wye, eastward from the border at Clifford, near his beloved Clyro, across the river in Powys. Though most of his diaries were written in earlier days in Welsh Clyro, there is 'Kilvert country' in Herefordshire too, from Clifford to Dorstone, Staunton-on-Wye, Mansell Gamage and Byford. Most of his journeys were made on foot, 'walking the villages'. On 22 April 1876, he 'walked up to the top of Moccas Park, whence we had a glorious view of the Golden Valley, shining in the evening sunlight, with the white houses of Dorstone scattered about the green hillsides'. Kilvert's love of nature and particularly of trees is evident. In the garden of Monnington Rectory he recalled 'the tallest, largest, stateliest ash ...' and 'a great grey tower' of oak at Moccas Court.

Kilvert was a railway enthusiast. He enjoyed train journeys and found the new Midland line from Hereford to Hay-on-Wye, opened in 1864, useful for his work and pleasure. In 1874 he had to 'scamper back to Whitney Rectory to catch the 1.08 train to Hay Castle'. Whitney church is full of memorials to the family of Tomkyns Dew, whom Kilvert was visiting. The flight of wooden steps down which he might have 'scampered' still leads steeply from the Court to the deserted railway station. It is sad that the station at Kinnersley is now derelict. Only an imaginative eye can share Kilvert's pleasure when, in July 1878, he drove with his father to Kinnersley station in

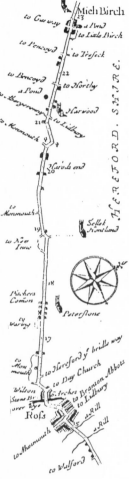

Extract from Road Atlas of John Ogilby, 1765

Baynham's trap and went by the 9.50 train to Talyllyn, to fish in Llangorst Lake. On 13 March 1879 he 'walked with Sam to catch the 11.45 train to Hereford' – a convenience which many Herefordshire folk would welcome today.

The image of an impoverished Victorian parson in a lean and hungry state is quickly dispelled. Kilvert records many treats. At the Tithe Audit and dinner held in the vicarage in February 1878, the business of tithes seems to have been secondary to the refreshments. The farmers 'regaled themselves with bread and cheese, some of them eating and drinking the value of the tithe they had paid'. The dinner which followed was 'a very noble turkey'; at the foot of the table was roast beef, at the sides jugged hare and beefsteak pie, preceded by pea-soup and, in due course, followed by plum pudding, apple tart, mince pies, blancmange, cheese and dessert. Kilvert adds modestly 'I think that they enjoyed themselves'.

Kilvert's style, and his bearded visage, give an impression of a man much older than his years. Sadly, his marriage to Elizabeth Rowland was only five weeks old when he died of peritonitis, aged thirty-eight. His memory is kept very green in the ancient church of St Andrews in Bredwardine.

Finally, we come to a time of living memory. Still a useful guide to Herefordshire, Arthur Mee's book in the *King's England* series is doubly interesting in offering a comparison with a 'then' which, incredibly for some of us, is now half-a-century ago. Mee's *Herefordshire* is full of descriptions 'for those who tire of the spoiling of our countryside, who would see it as it has been for generation after generation, before the twentieth century came with its charabancs and bungalows. Here is a county of their choice, green fields and quiet places, rivers and valleys and hills, time moving slowly, and beauty and tranquillity the world has not destroyed'. This was Yatton in 1938:

> Here in a sleepy hollow is an old farm, with a cider mill where a horse still draws the roller to crush the apples. By the farm is a deserted Norman chapel, crowned by a 16th-century timbered belfry. It has a fine doorway, with a zigzag on its arch as the Normans left it, with a sprig of foliage carved in its tympanum, and inside, the battered bowl of a Norman font. Half a mile away is an old thatched post office and a 19th-century church looking over farms, cottages and orchards to the Malvern Hills ...

There is now no hamlet, only widely-spaced and prosperous farms. At Chapel Farm, the Norman chapel still stands, well-roofed as a redundant church, the font and the piscina still in place, the zigzag door-arch and its tympanum intact. The broken cider-mill is now a flower-bed, the horse is long gone. The thatched post office is no more, but the 19th-century church – locked against vandals –

overlooks the same view: only the cottages are missing. The church is now part of the parish of Much Marcle; its last burial was in 1978. Like Ullingswick since its enclosure, Yatton has fallen victim to more intensive farming.

More recently, in 1977 a Herefordshire headmaster-historian wrote a description which, for any of us who have arrived at evening in a Herefordshire market town, revives memories which cannot be better described than by J.W. Tonkin, in his *Herefordshire*:

> The writer and his wife first saw Herefordshire on a bitter January afternoon during the snow and frost of the winter of 1963. They drove into the county from the east across the river Teme and up the hill over Bringsty Common, past the woods of Brockhampton to Bromyard. In those days, before the by-pass was built, the road ran through the main street where the lights were going up and the black-and-white of the timber-framed houses seemed to belong to the snow-covered landscape. It was warm and welcoming.

That indeed was – and still is – Herefordshire.

XVII Enclosure of the Fields

The traditional pattern of Herefordshire's early field-systems is uncertain. We look in vain for a widespread 'three-field-system'. There are some traces of open fields in Herefordshire, but they are not as numerous as elsewhere, nor did they survive as long. Scattered strips were gradually redistributed and enclosed for greater convenience, as manorial customs died out. In some counties, enclosure took place in one drastic reorganisation, to accommodate Tudor sheep-ranching, or 18th-century improvements. In Herefordshire, the process was one of piecemeal exchange between neighbours over several centuries. A core of open arable, or a fringe of common pasture, might remain unfenced for generations, diminished by the growth of more compact farms. There are often 'ancient enclosures' on Herefordshire enclosure maps, but little surviving manorial record of their gradual change. None of Herefordshire's manorial rolls and registers have been published.

Hop kilns

Survivals of medieval strips can be sought, fossilised in the ground as 'ridge and furrow', which curves through more recent hedges. On old maps these strips appear in ancient field-names – 'ridges, furlongs, lengths and butts'. Ridge and furrow is not as conspicuous in Herefordshire as in Leicestershire or Warwickshire, but we find some significant field-names in 19th-century tithe maps. We must turn to the useful, though late, parliamentary enclosure documents to find the few villages which still had open arable fields to enclose. These date from 1779 (at Winforton) to 1863 (at Moseley). Another 50 enclosure acts, like Marden's or Wigmore's, refer only to the enclosure of rough pasture, woodland, commons and wasteland. Some awards contain scanty references to a few scattered strips, but very few of these are accompanied by an explicit map.

In the south-west of the county, a Celtic tradition of small pastoral holdings with scattered hamlets set a different pattern of fields to that of Saxon ploughlands and nucleated villages. The county's afforested area, too, would not lend itself to extensive clearance. We have seen in Domesday how many waste manors had reverted to hunting grounds. Very small parishes, nibbled from the forest, could never have had large open-fields; in some places steep contours could only be ploughed piecemeal. Nor was the county's long tradition of

95

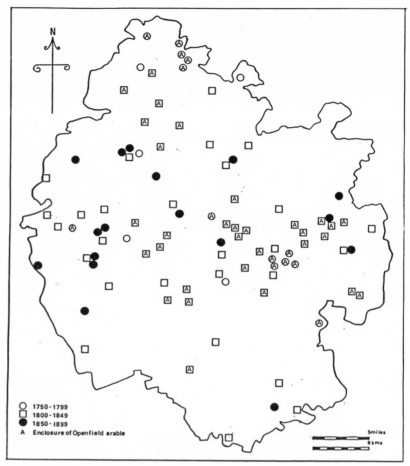

14. Distribution of Enclosures.

Legend (on map):
○ 1750-1799
□ 1800-1849
● 1850-1899
Ⓐ Enclosure of Openfield arable

5 miles
8 kms

sheep-farming, or the widespread plantation of orchards and hopyards conducive to the development of open-field farming.

Herefordshire has many scattered settlements made up of separate 'townships'; each hamlet produced its own field pattern or cluster of enclosed farms. Medieval increase in population might result in colonisation of new fields, but these often fell back into disuse in later recession. An excavation report on a deserted village site at Tedstone Wafer 'showed a number of medieval buildings, interpreted as the remains of a nucleated settlement that was deserted, on pottery evidence, in the 13th or 14th century'. There were traces of a typical medieval village street and some evidence of ridge and furrow in the fields. In Domesday this is recorded as a Lacy manor, with one plough in demesne. The excavation report lists 21 similar deserted medieval sites in places which are no longer nucleated villages. Their grass-grown mounds suggest that early nucleated villages *did* exist in Herefordshire; they also imply that many were soon dispersed.

96

36. Leintwardine stands at a vital bridging-point, where the river Clun joins the Teme and the main north–south and east–west roads cross the river. Here was the Roman military depot of *Bravonium* and Francis Brett Young's 'Lesswardine'.

37. This fragment of the original wall stands by Eign Gate, Hereford. From here, along Newmarket Street to Bath Street, the circuit has been carefully made.

38. Many of Hereford's abandoned railway stations have been converted to domestic uses. This halt was at Carey on the GWR line from Ross to Hereford, on the Ballingham–Holme Lacy section, which is still accessible to walkers.

39. Yatton, near Ross, is a deserted village with two churches. This redundant Norman chapel, with its fine door, is found in a farmyard. The 19th-century church stands on a hill half a mile away.

40. Moccas Court with its mellow brick facade stands in its park, by a stand of ancient oaks, which Kilvert described in 1876 as 'grey old men of Moccas . . . [which] look as if they had been at the beginning and making of the world and will probably see its end'.

41. Dinmore Manor seen from the parapet of the cloisters, with the medieval chapel of the Hospitallers on the right.

42. Eign Gate pedestrian precinct in Hereford, looking towards All Saints. It was said that the vista along every street in the city looked towards a church.

43. A well-known view of Church Lane in Ledbury, which leads to the detached 13th-century church tower and its 18th-century spire. The lane once ran alongside the village green of Saxon *Liedeberge*. It now houses a remarkable range of timbered buildings, including the 15th-century Grammar School and *Prince of Wales* inn.

The 16th-century survival of a three-field system at Stoke Prior, in Humber and Risbury, is mapped by H.L. Gray from 'two carefully drawn plans' of enclosed open strips. Gray also illustrates the common fields of Holmer, enclosed in 1855; 16 fields are named, their average size no more than 20 to 30 acres. Marden too, enclosed in 1819, had large areas of old enclosures surrounding 46 fields and patches, 'distributed like islands throughout the entire area of the parish'. Such numerous 'fields' are typical of many Herefordshire enclosures – 13 at Much Cowarne, 30 at Madley, 40 at Much Marcle.

A Tudor survey of seven villages belonging to the abbey of Wigmore, including Letton, Adforton, Yatton and Lye tabulates messuages, old enclosures, common meadow and the distribution of arable acres in the open fields. These ranged from holdings of 10 to 60 acres, with a few smallholdings of two and a half to six acres. Little of this open land remained to be enclosed in the 19th century; 1,200 acres had been reduced, piecemeal, to three hundred. We cannot place Herefordshire's 'old enclosure' more precisely than about the 17th century, for W.E. Tate finds no evidence of Tudor depopulation by enclosure comparable with that in the Midlands.

Parliamentary enclosure began late in Herefordshire. Most of the county's 76 enclosure acts were passed between 1800 and 1849. Enclosures form a broad belt across the centre of the county, with an early group of arable awards to the north, around Kingsland and Wigmore. There are similar concentrations to the east of Hereford, around Bishops Frome, Stoke Edith and Marden. There is a marked absence of parliamentary enclosure south of a line from Eastnor (enclosed in 1816), to Michaelchurch Escley (enclosed in 1852), with Orcup (1814) as an exceptional arable example in the south. Archenfield was already, as Leland noted, 'full of enclosures'. The entire area of Herefordshire open to parliamentary enclosure was relatively small, some 2,500 acres, with an average of about 150 acres to each award. This represents only about four per cent of the county's land.

Hereford cattle

A few of the later awards contain valuable evidence of the nature of enclosure and its implications for the villagers. At Ullingswick we find the unusual case of a village whose tithe map (1839) is *earlier* than the enclosure plan of 1856. The earlier document preserves an unusually clear picture of the 290 acres of open cultivation in Bebury Field, Broomhill Field and Wood Field. By contrast, the Ordnance Survey map of 1902 shows that the numerous small 'lengths' on the west and south-east boundaries of the parish have merged into larger fields, of which only the curving boundaries of Broomhill Field can still be seen. Elsewhere, in Bebury Field to the north-west and Wood Field to

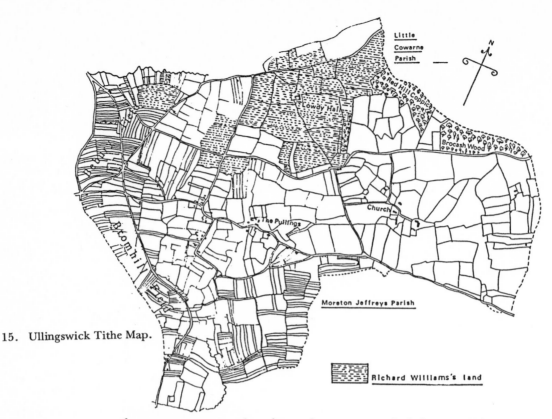

15. Ullingswick Tithe Map.

the east, open strips have been overruled by straight surveyor's divisions. A few fossilised strips survive, often as orchards. Most of the village's fields are flat pasture, with no trace of ridge and furrow.

The motive of the enclosers was 'improvement'. At Tarrington, 12 open-fields containing upwards of four hundred and fifty acres, lay 'inter-mixed and dispersed in small parcels, inconveniently situated in respect of their several proprietors and in their then state incapable of any considerable improvement'. Mr. Edward Foley received 17 allotments in nine of the arable fields; his allocation was 168 acres – half the total award. For this he paid £855. Twelve owners shared 326 acres of enclosed arable and meadow. One or two villagers were awarded three roods each, for which they paid up to £5 each. There was little profit in enclosure for the smallholder, or for the tenant who lost his lease.

Much Marcle, enclosed in 1797, produces an unusual series of estate papers which reveal the behind-the-scenes negotiations for enclosure. Edward Wallwyn had come into the inheritance of 'Hellens', the second largest estate in the village, a complex of ten farms totalling 800 acres. Some of his land lay in the 600 acres of open-fields, a small portion of the 4,600-acre parish, and small inconvenience to a wealthy man. Wallwyn, however, was concerned

98

about the encroachments of an increasing number of landless labourers. As squire, he objected to their 'hog-stye' cottages, their dependence upon poor relief, their benefits of common and their rights-of-way across 'his' land.

Having repossessed 700 acres of his estate by exchange and purchase, Wallwyn set out to persuade his wealthy neighbours of the benefits of enclosure. Employing professional enclosure commissioners to survey and estimate for him, he overrode all opposition, claiming the greater good of the village as a whole. The necessary consent of the four-fifths of the landowners was never gained, only 80 per cent of the *value* of the larger estates. Wallwyn and his friends found it easy to 'suppress' smallholders who tried 'to throw a damp on our proceedings'. Meetings were advertised in the *Herefordshire Times*, but many sessions were held at a distance from the village, at Ledbury, Upton-on-Severn and Tewkesbury. Objections were skilfully explained away by the commissioners, and parliamentary approval was gained within a year of Mr. Wallwyn's first move.

The results of enclosure in Much Marcle were not dramatic. There was no change to the landscape, and any hardship was on a small scale for small people. In all there were 95 allotments; almost half of these were less than three acres in extent. Seventy per cent of the enclosed area went in five lots of over two hundred acres each. One smallholder refused his award of 21 acres; another was ordered to accept £5 5s compensation for the loss of his lease. At 16s 6d an acre, charges for enclosure were relatively higher for the small awards, to which must be added the costs of fencing. Within a year, distress warrants were being served on those who could not find money to pay their arrears. 'Hellens' acquired 156 small lots of 185 acres in all. To those who had, more was given. In 1941, there were eleven farmers with over one hundred and fifty acres; in 1797 there had been only four with over a hundred. The village inn is called the *Wallwyn Arms Hotel*.

Most of these Herefordshire villages are today more 'enclosed' than they were in 1840. There is no village now at Ullingswick; the main street is a cul-de-sac, shop and inn are on the outskirts. All the enclosure roads, clearly marked on the 1901 Ordnance Survey map, are now stopped up by one means or another; the farms are large and prosperous limited companies. In the churchyard, moved to the wall, are the gravestones of the farmers named in the enclosure award, the Skerretts, Williams and Manns. These are, apparently, their only memorial in a village which no longer exists.

XVIII Canals, Turnpikes and Stage Coaches

Eighteenth-century industrial revolution was a hit-and-miss affair. In the 17th and 18th centuries, in some rural counties like Shropshire and Lancashire, inventive men of vision won a series of industrial gambles with raw materials, skills, water-power and transport, which promised early success. Industrial gamblers like Yarranton in Worcestershire made vigorous attempts to revolutionise 17th-century production by experiments with power and transport. Canals, water-wheel forges and railways were their inventions. Innovation was as often defeated by restrictive attitudes and lack of investment as by lack of natural resources.

Herefordshire lacked opportunists and too many of the county towns' experiments, especially with canals, failed. There were also industrial possibilities; Herefordshire *was* a manufacturing county in the 17th century. There were iron-works near Ross, with other furnaces and forges at Whitchurch, St Weonards, Peterchurch and Llancillo. Gloving was well established at Hereford, Ledbury, Leominster, Kington and Weobley. Above all, a rich clothiers' industry flourished in the county. During the 18th century there were paper mills at Mortimer's Cross and Ross; cotton spinning was introduced to Leominster in 1740, but the trade was short-lived. Industry might, with more inventiveness, have taken firm root in the county. For any more profitable production, the essential key was transport. The ability to move quantities of materials, fuel and products was, potentially, the most revolutionary factor of all.

The roads of Herefordshire were in a sad state of repair throughout the 17th and 18th centuries. Statute labour, organised by parish surveyors, did little more than repair the worst ravages of winter weather. One writer observed that, 'In winter the roads of Herefordshire are proverbial in England; they are such as one might expect to meet in the marshes of Holland or the mountains of Switzerland ... [they] are impassable to wagons and carts, though towards the end of April, the surface is levelled by means of ploughs drawn by 8 or 10 horses. The narrow forest roads and hollow ways still remain; in many places it is impossible for carriages to pass each other ... the lands in some parts of the county could be improved one quarter of their value by good roads. At present six or seven horses are necessary to drag a load to market.' It is not surprising that more

*Tollhouse near
Kington*

100

profitable improvement of the county's waterways was the first thought of engineers and investors.

In 1695 a county rate was levied by Act of Parliament to improve the navigation of the Wye from Monmouth to Hereford. Another Act intended to make the Lugg navigable from Lugwardine to Leominster, an endeavour which rewarded private subscribers with some success in 1714. There were repeated attempts to join Hereford to Gloucester, or Leominster to the Severn by means of canals. Villages to the east of the county, at Colwall, Pixley, Cradley and Marcle, which depended more upon the navigation of the Severn than the Wye, resisted the threat of Hereford's competition by river improvement. In spite of the frustration of so many enterprises, transport by water was still likely to be cheaper than road haulage, whilst coal came by pack-mule from Wales or Titterton Clee.

After several canal failures, it seemed that road improvement must offer an alternative. Local gentry and townsmen turned their attention for two generations to the passing of local Acts for the raising of Turnpike Trusts. In 1721, Ledbury nominated 39 trustees who set up toll-bars on all roads entering the town. Similar Acts followed for repairing the roads leading into Hereford in 1730 and 1749, 'which said roads by reason of the deep soil thereof, the many carriages and droves of cattle frequently passing through the same are become so ruinous and bad that many parts thereof are impassable in the winter season.' In spite of these efforts, by 1769 the same roads were still found to be 'very ruinous and almost impassable for travellers and carriages'. All the roads which radiate from Bromyard were covered by an Act of 1751. Leominster too, from 1729 to 1800, and Ross in 1791, looked to the same solution. There was an interesting development of a new road from Brecon via Hay, Whitney and Bredwardine Passage, which put several ferries out of business.

The immediate result of these Acts was to encircle each town with a ring of toll-bars and gates. Ross's radius was shortest, with improved stretches of road extending to Upton Bishop, Walford and Weston-under-Penyard. Leominster's ring of improvement extended for five miles, to Brimfield, Birley, Hope-under-Dinmore, Kingsland and Eardisland. Hereford's net was widest, radiating more than 10 miles, to St Weonards, Kentchurch, Dilwyn, Lea and Peterstow, Bredwardine and the bounds of the county. Lists of tolls are given, as for the roads into the city:

Coach, Berlin, Landau, Chariot, Hearse, Calash, Chaise	
or chair, drawn by 6 horses	1s. 6d.
Coach, Berlin etc. drawn by 4 horses	1s. 0d.
Coach, Berlin etc. drawn by fewer than 4 horses	6d.

KINGSWOOD GATE

Prees Floodgates, Hergest, Sunset, Headbrook, Moseley Crossway, Titley. Avenue Next-end. Lyonshall and Eardisley, Gates & Bars

Horse
Waggon
Cart
Gig
Chaise
Cattle
Sheep
Pigs
Asses

187

Poster: scale of tolls

101

For every horse drawing a wagon, wain or cart	3d.
Ox or neat cattle carrying grain or straw, hay or fodder, dung or lime for the improvement of land	2d.
Horse, mule, ass, laden or unladen, unless employed to carry charcoal to any Ironworks	1d.
Every drove of oxen, cows or neat cattle, per score	10d.
Every drove of calves, hogs, sheep or lambs, per score	5d.

Milestone

Milestone

Tolls were taken once for each day's journey; there was no payment on stone or gravel for repairing roads, nor on corn for the mill, on cattle going to water, or on horses for shoeing. The Royal Mail and soldiers on the march were exempt, also official vehicles removing vagrants from the parish, or any carriage concerned with elections. Church-goers, funerals and clergy visiting the sick paid no tolls. Charges at Leominster and Ross were similar, though cattle on the hoof paid twice the city rate.

Surveyors were appointed to dig gravel, stone and sand from the commons, or from private land on payment. They could remove 'nuisances', such as dung, ashes and rubbish from the roadway, cut down trees and hedges and insist that all farm gates opened off the road. Milestones and sign-posts were to be erected, and the penalty for defacement was 40s. For the first time, the statute mile became standard, replacing rural variations. Even now, 'Herefordshire miles' seem longer than others to the walker, just as they did to Celia Fiennes in 1696.

The responsibilities of the Trusts did not cancel the longstanding requirement of statute work. Lists of inhabitants liable for road-making and carting of materials were to be supplied to the Trusts' surveyors by parish surveyors, overseers of the poor or church-wardens, with heavy penalties for negligence. Appeals could be taken to Quarter Sessions by 'persons aggrieved'. Many were in fact aggrieved to the point of riot and civil insurrection punishable by death.

The network of toll-bars and gates erected by the several Trusts in Herefordshire can be traced on the first edition of the county's one-inch Ordnance Survey sheets of 1831-2, each marked *TP*. Occasionally, a toll-house survives, as at Kington, or a cottage named 'Turnpike House' as on the A4103 on Fromes Hill. A few of the old milestones survive, clearly marked on the OS sheets for 1832 and 1984; only a few are turnpike stones, many have been replaced by later authorities. The actual course of each road, though much improved by widening and straightening of bends, follows almost identical routes in most cases and can be easily followed on the ground today. In a few cases, particularly on difficult hills, the motor-road is

102

diverted from an abandoned stretch of coach road, as on Dinmore Hill.

The Trusts did too little to make lasting improvements of road surfaces or reduce the cost of transport. Attention turned once again to the prospects of profitable canal transport, Ledbury taking the lead to become the only market town with a successful canal development and coal wharfs on New Street. Soon the continuing demand for swifter carriage would lead to more adventurous experiments – tramways from Abergavenny and Brecon, or Captain Radford RN's steamboat packet *Paul Pry*, plying from Hereford to Chepstow during the 1820s. Yet, for one last golden age, at the beginning of the 19th century, turnpike roads made stage-coach travel a profitable undertaking.

On any weekday in 1830, as many as 40 stage-coaches rattled in and out of the cobbled yards of the *Green Dragon*, *City Arms* or *Black Swan* hotels in Hereford. Gaudy in canary yellow or bright scarlet, each coach stood eight feet tall, with a team of four-in-hand, a well-wrapped coachman, 12 passengers up and six inside, with a uniformed guard sounding 'Clear-the-road' on a yard of tin post-horn or warbling 'Annie Laurie' on his key-bugle. Coaches with adventurous names – *Hero*, *Champion*, *Defiance* and *Tally Ho!* were run competitively by rival firms of owners. Fastest and smartest of all were the *Royal Mails*, in their black-and maroon livery with scarlet wheels, bearing the royal arms on their doors, their guards in scarlet coats. Each coach was 11 feet long with a wheel base of six feet six inches, and unladen weight of 18 cwt.

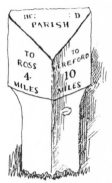

Milestone

The *Feathers* at Ledbury, the *Red Lion* at Leominster, the *Falcon* at Bromyard, *The Swan* at Ross, all shared in the brisk timetable and profits of up-to-date public transport. From five in the morning until midnight the teams were changed, the passengers breakfasted and dined, the mails and parcels taken aboard. Hereford can be seen on maps as being in a crucial position, as the hub of a widespread wheel of coach-roads radiating through Leominster, Hay, Monmouth, Ledbury, Bromyard and Presteign, to the far limits of London, the Midlands and west Wales. The main Herefordshire coach-roads were not merely a local service, but trans-county routes, running from outside Herefordshire and mostly measured from the *Bolt-in-Tun* in Fleet Street, with minor 'cross-roads' for local services.

There were in all some 20 different coach routes out of the city, with five different coach services to London and others to Bristol, Liverpool, Abergavenny, Aberystwyth, Milford Haven, Gloucester and Birmingham. Leominster was a second coaching centre, with its own more northerly routes into Wales via Kington and Rhayader and

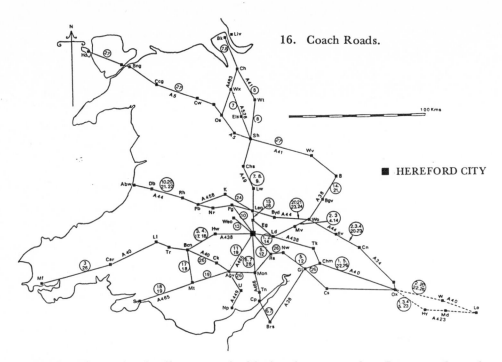

16. Coach Roads.

100 Kms

■ HEREFORD CITY

to London via Ledbury and Cheltenham, or by Bromyard and Worcester. Ross, too, maintained separate services other than those from Hereford, advertising its own London to Carmarthen route via Oxford, Cheltenham, Gloucester and Monmouth, thus offering an alternative to the uncomfortable Severn crossing into south Wales. Most of the coaches' highways are now modern motor roads – the A49, A465 and A438 are some examples.

The coaches aimed for a consistent speed of ten mph, but this varied from six to 12 mph according to the state of each stretch of road. A team of four could pull at full stretch for up to an hour non-stop between stages which are still marked by inns with stable yards at remarkably regular 10-mile intervals along the modern roads. Coach owners recruited retired servants from local houses to staff the coaching inns and many a deserted roadside hamlet must have existed solely for the benefit of the coaches. Stops for meals were cut to a minimum and an efficient team of guard and ostlers could change a team in 45 seconds, comparable with a racing motorist's pit-stop. As a result of such precision, villagers could set their watches by the coaches' passage.

The timetable of the nightly journey of the *Royal Mail* from Bristol, as it ran from the *City Arms* in Hereford to the *Saracen's Head* in Liverpool, completed the distance of 109 miles in 16 hours' travelling time in 1830:

104

City Arms, Hereford	11.15 p.m.	
Red Lion, Leominster	1.00 a.m.	12¾ miles
The Crown, Ludlow	3.00 a.m.	10 miles
The Crown, Church Stretton	4.30 a.m.	15¾ miles
The Lion, Shrewsbury	6.00 a.m.	13 miles
Bridgwater Arms, Ellesmere	8.00 a.m.	16¼ miles
The Wynnstay Arms, Wrexham	9.00 a.m.	11¾ miles
The Saracen's Head, Liverpool	3.15 p.m.	17½ miles

The Gloucester-Aberystwyth Mail

Coaches' names, their times of arrival and departure and the inns they served are found in the commercial directories of Kelly and Pigot under each main town. Coach owners also advertised regularly in the local press, claiming speed, safety and economy of fares. 'New, elegant, patent, speedy, safe and well-appointed' were the advertising slogans of the coaching age. By 1835, there were 700 mail coaches in service and several thousand stage coaches. As times were cut, so fares were reduced, often as loss-leaders impossible to sustain. In 1834, Jobson Morris & Co offered a record-breaking service on the Liverpool route, advertising 'Hereford to Liverpool in 12 hours!' – with 'no furious driving'. Competitive racing of coach against coach was a popular but dangerous sport, causing frequent, spectacular accidents and loss of life. Gray & Co's *Champion* travelled the 138 miles from London to Hereford via High Wycombe, Oxford and Gloucester in 20 hours, an average seven mph. Their *Mazeppa* (named after Byron's heroic Polish Cossack) was faster, covering the slightly longer journey via Slough and Maidenhead in 17 hours.

A side effect of regular London services was the fast transmission of news. At the height of the Reform Bill crisis in 1832, coachmen were selling copies of the London newspapers in Ross for £2 each. Bayzard, guard on the *Mazeppa*, was carried shoulder-high into the Herefordshire political club and was paid £5 for his copies of the *Times*, which brought news of the passage of the Bill. Copies of the newspaper were framed and hung in the club-room.

Ironically, the coaching service reached its peak performance exactly at the time when the railways began to offer the challenge that would make coaches obsolete and empty the roads until the invention of motor-cars, which would in their turn remove passengers and freight from the rails. In Herefordshire, the Shrewsbury to Hereford railway was opened in 1854. Constructed at a cost of £628,810 and paying a dividend of five per cent, the railway followed the north-south coach road as precisely as the turnpike followed its Roman ancestor, crossing and re-crossing the modern A49 along its whole 51 miles. The days of the stage-coach were numbered; for a while it really was The Age of the Train.

105

XIX Victorian Villages

Commercial directories of the 19th century are a familiar source of useful information about Victorian communities. An especially interesting mid-19th-century example is Edward Cassey's *Directory of Herefordshire*, published in 1858. Cassey describes about 250 towns and villages, giving each place's situation and communications, whether by turnpike road or new railway line, and its administrative districts. The principal landowners are listed, along with the acreage of each parish, the nature of its soil, crops and local industry. Population figures are taken from the 1851 census, with details of church, schools, chapels, charities and items of antiquarian interest. This information is followed by a selective list of farmers, shopkeepers and craftsmen in each village, with names of farms, but no other addresses. A commercial directory of this type is not complete, nor statistically sound, but it offers a wealth of information which offers many leads to other documents.

Yatton's cider mill — flowerbed

In his Introduction, Cassey describes a mainly agricultural county, cultivating grain, cider and hops and rearing cattle. There is usually one farmer named for approximately 200 acres of each parish. Manufactures were rare, apart from some small-scale cloth-making and gloving. Coal mining occupied some 230 men, quarrying 70 and brickmaking 200. Most local 'mechanics' were carpenters, wheelwrights, masons and blacksmiths.

Cassey points out that internal waterways were not extensive; there were canals only from Ledbury to Gloucester and from Leominster to Tenbury. 'Except by means of the Wye to Chepstow and the Bristol Channel, Herefordshire is wanting in communication by water.' Railways were an innovation, with the Shrewsbury-Hereford line newly opened and 'a railway from Hereford to Worcester about to be constructed'. Cassey places most villages in relation to the nearest turnpike road, stage-coach route or carrier's journey.

Villages ranged in size from a few hundred acres (Brobury 442, Stretford 424 etc.) to more than 5,000 at Abbey Dore, Dilwyn and Madley; 60 per cent of Herefordshire parishes were smaller than 2,000 acres. Their populations, in proportion, ranged from fewer than 100 to more than 1,000 inhabitants and, in most cases, were about four times their present size. The average village had no more than 300

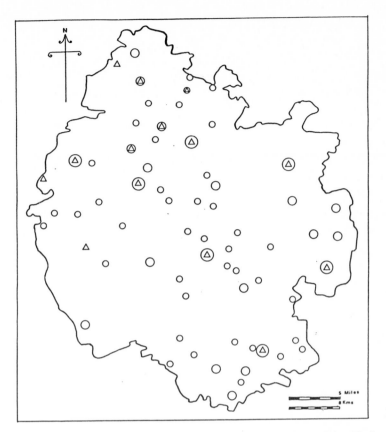

17. Village Distribution.

souls and there were about a dozen hamlets, like Bolstone Dewsall and Willersley, with fewer than 100 inhabitants.

Among the greater landowners, each holding in several villages, were the Foleys of Stourbridge, the Bishop of Hereford, the Governors of Guy's Hospital, the industrialist Arkwright and the Earl of Abergavenny, with his extensive manor of Ewias Lacy. Other influential gentry were Colonel Scudamore and Sir Hungerford Hoskyns, lords of the manor in several villages; Colonel Vaughan at Welsh Bicknor, Tomkyns Dew at Whitney, Colonel Biddulph at Burghill and the Cornewalls at Moccas.

Herefordshire's average village in 1858 housed about 250 people living in 50-60 houses. Many are described as 'straggling' or 'scattered' villages with about 30 hamlets of no more than 100 people listing no occupation other than farming. Otherwise, every village street provided at least one general store, an inn, a shoemaker, carpenter, wheelwright and blacksmith, and a church school. Butchers' shops were rare, as each farmer butchered his own meat for sale. Village bakers are almost non-existent in Cassey; most women baked their family bread. Village dressmakers and milliners are also

107

absent; Garway and Harewood have two exceptions. A tailor was found in every second or third village, but ironmongers' wares were found either at the general store or at the blacksmith's forge. Only about one village in three housed a Post Office as yet, and letters were fetched by carrier or 'foot-post' from the nearest town, sometimes, as in the case of Peterchurch or Rowlstone, from as far as Hereford, 12 miles away.

Towns like Ledbury, Bromyard, Weobley, Leominster, Ross and Kington housed upwards of 5,000 people. Here were the courts, magistrates, Boards of Guardians, Union workhouses and regular weekly markets. Their streets were lighted by gas and thoroughly 'improved'; some, like Bromyard, Kington and Ledbury, published a weekly newspaper. As agricultural centres, these towns provided the services of auctioneers, land-agents, corn-factors, cattle-dealers, veterinary surgeons, insurance agents, lawyers and tax collectors. There was also a small collection of industries rarely found outside the towns. At Bromyard, for example, we find a wool-stapler, tin-man, tanner, saddlers and earthenware dealers.

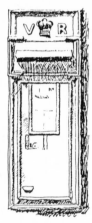

Victorian postbox

The range of retail shops also confirms 'township' status. Bromyard in 1858 had not only 18 grocers, but also 10 innkeepers, 11 drapers or tailors and six shoemakers; these we find, in smaller numbers, in any village. Towns also provided the wares of newsagents, stationers, hairdressers, watchmakers, ironmongers, bakers and chemists. A few middle-sized places, like Fownhope, Ewias Harold, Peterchurch and Longtown, could boast exceptional examples of rural chemists' shops, usually in place of a doctor; Weobley and Leintwardine had druggists and other trades in a small town centre. Walford is an exceptional village in accommodating a pastry-cook, as is Holmer with its wine-and-spirits merchant, or Bredwardine with a clock-maker. Some places, with populations between 1,000 and 2,000, are too large to be seen as villages, but too small to become towns. Of these, Leintwardine (pop:1606) and Pembridge (1319) are good examples of larger market-villages or declining market-towns. To these, we might add Fownhope (1059), Bodenham (1113), Llangarron (1217) and Walford (1807).

Prosperity in a few larger places was due to a localized industry. Aymestry had limestone quarries, Fownhope a silk-throwing mill, and at Lugwardine there were extensive brick-works. In places like Llangarron, which housed as many as 10 shoemakers and 12 carpenters, these must have constituted some sort of cottage industry. Village centres are often identified by a concentration of building workers, masons and timber-merchants, a feature still found in many larger Herefordshire villages.

The larger industrial villages were often the centres of dissenting communities, with chapels for Baptists, Primitive Methodists and Independents. At Fownhope there was a meeting-house for the Plymouth Brethren and a Baptist chapel; at Colwall there were two meeting-houses for Dissenters 'who are becoming numerous'. Another feature of these places is the siting of one or more mills. Coincidentally, Cassey lists an almost identical number of mills as the 71 of Domesday Book, though the 1861 census tabulates 281 millers. Many of these mills, as at Bishops Frome, Bodenham, Bosbury, Linton, Monkland, Stoke Lacy and Wellington, were still on their Domesday sites. Llangarron and Leintwardine had four mills each and Eardisland had three.

Hereford-Shrewsbury line train

There are at least a score of villages which, though smaller, with about 750 people, were evidently retail centres for their neighbourhood. The sign of these centres is usually a butcher's shop or post office. They also offered more of the usual village tradesmen, though none of the more exotic urban crafts. At places like Eardisley (pop:811), Mordiford (677), Weston-under-Penyard (733) and Garway (590), we find four, five or even seven general stores, two or three tailors, three or four shoemakers. Almost every village had its inn, but some of those with about 750 people are likely to offer two or three hostelries, as well as beer or cider sellers.

In the smaller retail centres there was no industry other than occasional craftsmen, makers of rope, baskets, harness, hurdles or bricks, with an occasional timber-merchant. At Whitchurch there was a boat-builder and a cabinet-maker; at Mordiford, Lugwardine and Orleton we find some nailers. Other unusual trades include an occasional wood-turner (Woolhope), coal-dealer (Peterstow), weavers (Pipe & Lyde and Staunton-on-Arrow), tanners (Wolferlow) and a fishing tackle maker at Kingsland. In the 'village centres' there were, however, larger numbers of village crafts – two or three wheelwrights, three or four blacksmiths and as many as six carpenters in villages like Linton, Goodrich, Mordiford and Weston-under-Penyard. Most small places kept one shoemaker busy; there were four at Lyonshall and Eardisley; Mordiford, Peterchurch and Orleton each had three.

Almost every Herefordshire village, large or small, had its school in 1858. The village centres, like the small towns, are likely to have had two or three, including an Elizabethan grammar school or other ancient foundation, as at Bosbury, Eardisland and Colwall. There also may be almshouses there, as at Wellington and Pembridge. A village post office, recently opened at Much Marcle in 1856, is another sign of status, as is the innovation of a railway station at Kingsland, Eye and St Devereux. Village veterinary surgeons were rarely recorded by

Cassey; there was one at Lea and another at Whitney. Only one thatcher is listed, but this illustrates the incompleteness of directories, as the 1861 census tables number 24 'vets' in the county and 68 thatchers. Doctors were really scarce; there are only 81 surgeons and physicians listed by the census for the whole county. Exactly 100 years later, there were 200 doctors. Cassey names about one doctor in every six villages, often as the official poor-law surgeon. Doctors' practices tended to group together in towns; often, they occurred in a village only by accident of residence or retirement, rather than as a deliberate choice of rural practice.

All in all, we find in Cassey a reliable picture of Victorian places and people in Herefordshire. Combined with additional data given in census returns, parish records, school log-books, photographs and newspapers, these Directories provide a powerful battery of sources for a study of Herefordshire in the mid-19th century. Using them, we can indeed re-populate the villages.

Inn sign — The Lion *at Leintwardine*

XX Recent History

In many a village, insulated from the thunder of heavy lorries on the main roads, the scene is timeless – until a jet-fighter roars overhead. Yet, change is there, beginning as early as the 18th century. Among the first deliberate 'improvements' was an Act of 1774, 'for paving, repairing and cleansing the streets and lanes of the city of Hereford and suburbs thereof and removing nuisances and annoyances therein'. A similar Act was passed for Leominster in 1808. With enclosures, turnpikes and Improvement Acts, progress came to Herefordshire.

In direct line of succession to the 18th-century Acts was the supplying of water, gas and electricity to the towns and villages, from the turn of the century well into the 1960s. The towns were first to organise these amenities, but Bromyard had no mains water until 1900 and Leominster no sewage plant until 1963. Hereford's City Electricity Supply Works was opened in 1899; the Leominster company was given its monopoly in 1912 and the borough had its first electrical street-lighting by 1935. The small towns' undertakings were soon taken over by larger companies like the Shropshire, Worcester and Staffordshire Electric Supply. Bromyard handed over its redundant equipment to Ledbury and Kington in 1929. A rural development programme did not begin until after nationalisation of the private companies, from 1947 to 1970.

Herefordshire is still an agricultural county, but fundamental changes began before 1940 as cornfields gave way to grassland. The balance has tended to fluctuate with changing incentives, market trends, automated farming and hop-wilt. In 1970 Herefordshire farmers cultivated 434,000 acres. Of these, just under 50 per cent was grassland, just over 50 per cent was arable, but cereal crops accounted for only half the arable land. Now insurance companies and other large investors own many farms, but their more intensive farming has not, as yet, uprooted the landscape.

From 1801 to 1971 the county's population doubled, interrupted by a decline from 1911 to 1931. The main change was in the remarkable expansion of the city of Hereford. The addition of 25,000 to the city's population almost exactly matches the county's growth from 1901-70. *Decennial Tables of Occupations* for 1861 and 1961 reveal the changing pattern. In 1861, there were 10,500 men and women over 15 years of

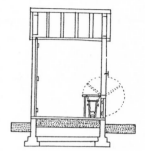

Privy closet, 1901

111

age in Herefordshire. Of these, 100 per cent of the men and nearly half the women were in work. More than half of them worked in agricultural crafts, including 5,000 women. Twenty per cent of the population were still employed in industries like leather-work, textiles, metal trades, stone-quarrying and wood-work. There was still some small-scale occupation of women in weaving flax, silk, lace and cotton. Women were also employed in making boots and gloves, but the massive female employment was in domestic service, millinery and shirt-making. Still the largest occupation was that of 17,000 male and female farm workers.

The greatest change in employment between 1861 and 1961 was the massive reduction of agricultural workers to only 23 per cent of the county's work force. This loss was intensified by a decline in allied trades, like millers, wheelwrights and corn dealers. Cottage industries, like weaving, nail-making and gloving had almost disappeared; thousands of shoemakers, masons and carpenters were also missing. The corresponding increase which mopped up the displaced 19th-century occupations were mainly electrical trades, transport, warehousing, clerical work, engineering, management and the invasion of the armed forces. Coachmen and carters were replaced by larger numbers of railwaymen and lorry drivers. There are now machinists and tool-makers instead of furnacemen and brass-founders; earth-movers are substitutes for hordes of navvies.

Women's work in 1961 was distributed over a wide range of occupations. Mostly they had moved into offices, as typists and telephonists, or became shop assistants, nurses, teachers and hairdressers. Cooks and housemaids have moved out of private houses, with their male counterparts, the grooms, coachmen, gardeners and footmen, but there were almost as many (5,000) classified in 1961 as 'maids and valets', cleaners, waitresses and kitchen hands as in 1861. These now work in hotels, offices and laundries, rather than in private 'service'.

A light-hearted indication of how the domestic scene has changed can be shown by making a courtship map. The marriage registers of any parish give the residence of each bridegroom, the bride usually being 'a spinster of this parish'. Registers for Woolhope from 1755 to 1812 are conveniently in print at the County Record Office. The maps show that in the 18th century Woolhope girls found their husbands almost entirely (98 per cent) within the county of Herefordshire. Two-thirds of the grooms lived within the village and another 22 per cent lived no more than five miles away. Only six husbands came from outside the county. Over a similar period, since the 1914-18 war, there was more mobility, though even today three-quarters of Woolhope's

GWR badge

112

18. Woolhope Courtship Map.

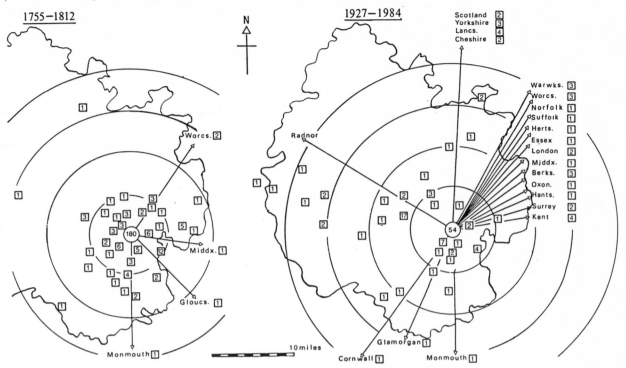

1755–1812

1927–1984

Scotland 2
Yorkshire 3
Lancs. 4
Cheshire 2

Warwks. 3
Worcs. 3
Norfolk 1
Suffolk 1
Herts. 1
Essex 1
London 2
Middx. 1
Berks. 3
Oxon. 1
Hants. 1
Surrey 2
Kent 4

Worcs. 2

Radnor

Middx. 1

Gloucs. 1

Glamorgan 1

Cornwall 1

Monmouth 1

Monmouth 1

10 miles

grooms are Herefordshire men. Those coming from inside the county are now more widely spaced and another 27 per cent come from outside Herefordshire.

The maps reveal the increasing lure of the city, six miles away, the invention of the bicycle and the peculiar convenience of the old Midland railway from Hay via Eardisley junction. It would take a local girl to explain the romantic associations of 18th-century Woolhope with Much Marcle, or why, with a solitary exception, no Woolhope girl accepts a suitor from Wales. Fifty per cent of the bridegrooms still live within five miles of the church.

Another way to investigate 19th-century households in village and town is to study the census enumeration books, available from 1841 to 1881, in the local libraries. House by house, Herefordshire's enumerators tabulated data about families, servants, lodgers and apprentices. In 1851 we find that Widemarsh Street was still largely inhabited by farmers and farm workers. Samuel Phelps, for example, a Gloucestershire man, farmed 100 urban acres with two labourers. A widower, his house was kept by a sister-in-law, Esther. She was helped by two maidservants; two boys aged 12, also entered as servants, might be the farm's two workmen. Most of Hereford's residents were born within the city or nearby villages; there was a strong Welsh contingent and many families came from Gloucester. Some came on

113

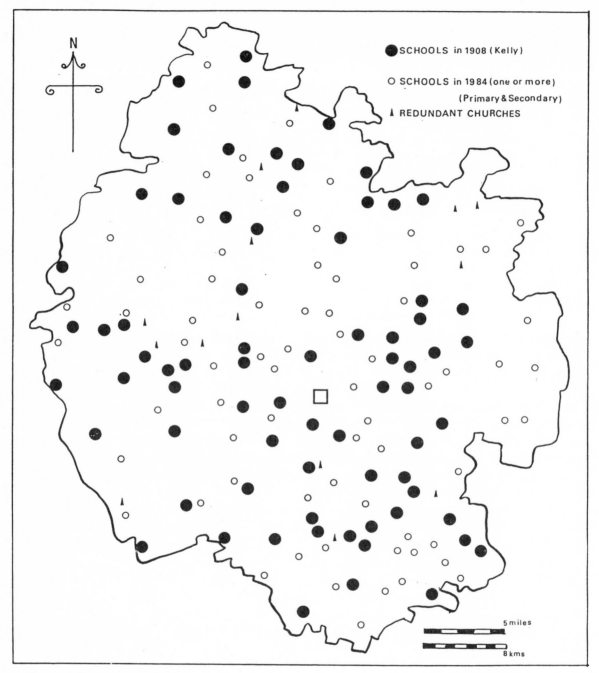

SCHOOLS in 1908 (Kelly)

SCHOOLS in 1984 (one or more)
(Primary & Secondary)

REDUNDANT CHURCHES

5 miles

8 kms

19. Schools and Churches.

the Hereford-Gloucester canal. In the canal basin, between Wide-marsh Street and Commercial Road, were moored seven narrow boats like the *Mary Ann* and *Trader*, each manned by three or four boatmen and their wives.

Broad Street in 1851 was crowded with shops and inns. Here were Ebenezer Child, music seller; Ann Lewis, maker of fishing tackle; Mary Jones at her Fancy Berlin Depository; and John Wilson, silk dyer. The shopkeepers' families lived over the shops, with a side entrance to the apprentices' lodgings. In 1881, Broad Street had similar shops and most of the same hotels; the *Green Dragon* was very busy. Evidently the courts were in session, as the guests included six barristers and a County Court judge, as well as the ubiquitous commercial traveller and an army sergeant-major. In addition to an Austrian waiter, the barmaid and ostler, there were seven maids and a waitress. A page, 15 years old, and a billiard-maker completed the hotel staff.

Down the street, Edwin Guy now kept the chemist's shop, employing his 18-year-old daughter as a second 'household servant'. Nicholas Harris owned the music shop, Ann Craggs a toy-shop. The most imposing emporium was Samuel E. Nash's draper's shop, with five assistants and an apprentice. There was a governess for the four children and the housework was done by Selina Careless and Martha Wargent, the housemaids. Most of these domestic servants came from Herefordshire villages or from Wales. Many of the tradesmen and apprentices were born farther afield in counties all over England. The most opulent household was the home of Canon William Peete Musgrave, a Londoner with three unmarried daughters. His wife Penelope's lady's maid, Sarah Glendenning, is notable for her daughter Alice, aged 16, who was a pupil-teacher, a generation before Hereford founded England's first local college for teachers in 1904. The Canon also employed a resident butler, footman, cook and three maids.

There had been an increase in Broad Street's public buildings since 1851. At Nos. 30-31 stood the Free Library; John Thornell (a 'superannuated postman') kept the Post Office at No. 22. The National Provincial Bank had opened a branch at Nos. 11-12; the banker, John A. Suter, was Captain in the 1st Herefordshire Volunteer Corps. His nephew was a lieutenant and another nephew was chief cashier. The bank also employed a resident pageboy, aged 15. Hereford was evidently busier since the opening of the railway station and the new market in the 1850s; indeed, the town was now expanding outside its ancient walls.

Sadly for Herefordshire, 'change' has too often meant 'loss', as more than a dozen redundant churches like Aconbury and Wormsley, or 74 closed Victorian schools like Kilpeck and Downton, testify. More potent has been the persistent reduction of the county's parliamentary representation. Two MPs were removed from the 'pocket borough' of Weobley in 1832; one of Leominster's members was lost in 1867, another in 1885; the county, in 1885, lost an MP gained by reform in 1832; and the city is now reduced to one MP. In all, the county and its towns have lost seven representatives in parliament.

No greater loss was ever suffered than that which all English counties experienced from 1914 to 1918. During the First World War, Herefordshire lost 2,000 of her menfolk in slaughter which exactly decimated the age group 18 to 45. *The Book of Remembrance* is full of their names, as are the sad, simple lists in every village church. Colwall lost 42 men, Holmer 65, Bromyard 43, Leominster 116, Ledbury 60 and more, and more. Lance-Corporal Alan Lewis, a Whitney man, was awarded a posthumous Victoria Cross. The county's other VC was W.C. Willis of HMS *Hussar*. He is listed amongst the city's 374 dead. After this cruel loss of potential teachers, poets, surgeons, politicians, writers, craftsmen and fathers, can we really believe that the county's life would ever be the same again?

In earlier years the county's military history was sporadic, the Herefordshire regiments repeatedly subjected to reorganization and disbandment. The 36th of Foot, Viscount Charlemont's Regiment, was raised in Ireland in 1701/2 as a marine corps. Its first battle honours list campaigns in the Peninsula and Hindestan, but the regiment was disbanded in 1881, amalgamated with the Worcestershire Regiment. During the Napoleonic Wars, a regiment of Herefordshire Volunteers was recruited; as the Militia it was disbanded in 1816. In 1859, the Herefordshire Rifle Volunteers were formed, including some Radnorshire companies. The Volunteers served in South Africa in 1900-02. In 1908, a 1st Battalion of the county's territorial force was raised to replace the Volunteer Corps. As The Herefordshire Regiment, the battalion went to war in 1914 and 1939, serving with distinction in Gallipoli, Palestine, Ypres and Falaise. From 1947 to 1967, this regiment became the Herefordshire Light Infantry and is now part of the 5th Light Infantry on call for NATO. The regiment's old barracks, built in 1856, is now the County Record Office, almost opposite *The Volunteer Inn* in Harold Street.

Some changes come quickly, but fail to last. Roman Kenchester and Leintwardine are monuments to regression, as are the county's many derelict railway lines. Railways were the most abortive agencies of

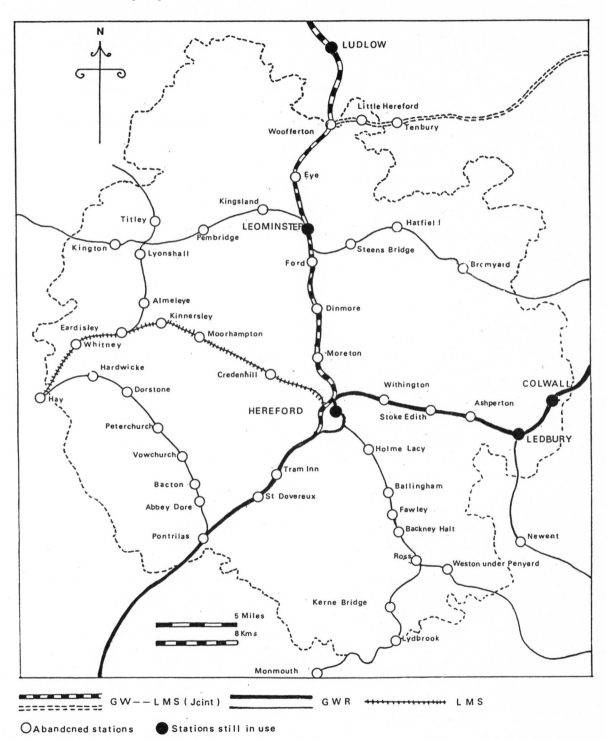

economic change in Herefordshire, because the city's strategic position in the railway age was seen only as a staging post between South Wales and Birkenhead, in the rivalry of GWR and LNWR for the Welsh coal freight. The first line to be opened ran from north to south; the Shrewsbury to Hereford railway was opened as a single line from Ludlow to Barrs Court Station in 1853. In 1861, a Worcester-Bromyard-Leominster company was founded, running five trains a day from Bromyard to Worcester, with excursions to London at less than 50p. The company faced financial problems and the Leominster line was not completed until 1897. An important item of freight was coal for the hop-kilns, with 5,000 Black Country folk as seasonal passengers to strip the hop-yards.

From Hereford, the lines were pushed southward by the Newport, Abergavenny and Hereford Company, later taken over by the West Midlands, or 'Werry Middling' Railway. In 1854, a double line was opened from Pontypool to Hereford, replacing three earlier tramways from Abergavenny. This line opened Hereford's second station, at Barton. In 1861, the line from Worcester first emerged from the Malvern tunnel at Colwall Stone, as part of the West Midlands Railway, joining the S. & H.R. at Shelwick, north of the city. South-westwards, in 1855, a single line was opened between Hereford, Ross and Gloucester. Another line to Hay and Brecon was opened by the MR in 1864, joining a GWR terminal at Eardisley and a third city station at Moorfields.

'Re-grouping', in 1921, shared Herefordshire's lines between the dominant GWR and the LMS. Today, three lines from Hereford survive, to Shrewsbury, Abergavenny and Gloucester. Other dismantled tracks run clearly across the Ordnance Survey maps into towns like Bromyard, Ross and Leominster, where the abandoned station yards are new industrial estates. Across the whole county, many an overgrown wayside halt, broken railway bridge or meaningless level-crossing take the walker unawares, in quiet lanes behind Eardisley and Norton Canon, or along Humber Brook from Stoke Prior to Hatfield and Bromyard. Surely one of the most beautiful abandoned railway tracks in Britain must be the old riverside line from Dorstone down the Golden Valley, to Abbey Dore and Ewias Harold?

It is the accessibility of motor roads which has done most to change the social pattern of many Herefordshire villages. *The Bromyard News and Record* reported its first fatal accident in August 1906, when the coroner expressed the county's attitude of 'awe and suspicion' towards all motorists. But attitudes change, with new concepts of 'commuter dormitories', 'light industry', 'school buses' and 'tourism'.

118

A rash of speculative building in places like Tarrington, Stoke Prior and Pencombe reflects their accessibility by motor car. More remote places, like Edvin Loach and Little Cowarne, represent a new phase of deserted villages.

Many of the county's industries are still closely linked with agriculture and natural resources. In many villages like Weobley, Eardisley, Wigmore or Leinthall Earls, we find small thriving engineering workshops for agricultural machinery, timber yards, quarries, tile-works, cider mills and furniture workshops. Elsewhere, production has spun off into prefabricated farmyard buildings, machinery and frozen poultry plants.

Cattle and sheep, fields and stone, orchards and timber are no longer Herefordshire's only means of production. During the post-war years, the Ministry of Defence perceived the economic and strategic potential of the county's remote situation. The strategies of the atomic age once again re-orientated the nation's defensive resources towards Herefordshire and the Marches. In 1980, Hereford's *Official Guide* recorded that, 'Much of Hereford's labour has of late been as varied as the Anglo-French Concorde, 'blank' coinage for decimalisation, refrigeration plant for Eastern Europe, transmission towers for the Nelson River Project in Manitoba, ball plug valves for over 70 countries and many other undertakings having great significance in our home and export markets'. Several of these industrial undertakings, sadly, have closed since 1980, but each of the smaller towns has its busy industrial estate.

Enough has been written elsewhere with deeply-felt passion about the anti-historical re-organisation of local government in 1972-4. The Act which dealt so arbitrarily with so many ancient towns and counties did not spare Herefordshire. The hotly resisted amalgamation of Hereford and Worcester lost long traditions of local government from the County Hall. The Districts which replaced the ancient borough of Leominster and the urban districts of Ross, Ledbury and Kington spread this unwanted change across the county. In Ledbury particularly, the awkward straddling of the Malvern Hills District aggravates local resentment of administration from another county.

Ironically, it seems as if resentment of 're-organisation' has, if anything, heightened Herefordshire's sense of identity, making its residents more conscious of their heritage. The reader is fortunate in that, as yet, this ancient county's historic records are safely kept in the old county town. For Herefordshire people, the past has a more desirable identity than the present.

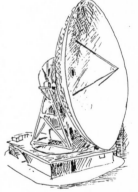

Madley Earth Station

119

Select Bibliography

TWNFC = Transactions of the Woolhope Naturalists' Field Club

Chapter I
Camden, William, *Britannia*, 1586 etc.
Fuller, H.V.L., *Herefordshire*, 1948
Kelly, E.R., *Post Office Directory of Shropshire, Herefordshire and Gloucestershire*, 1879
Kelly, E.R., 'Geology of Herefordshire ' in *Kelly's Directory of Herefordshire*, 1934
Mee, Arthur, *Herefordshire: (The King's England Series)*, 1938
Tonkin, J.W., *Herefordshire*, 1977
Tonkin, J.W., 'Jim and Muriel': *The Book of Hereford*, 1975
Victoria County History of Herefordshire, Vol. I, 1908, passim for Chapters I to VI

Chapter II
Anthony, I.E., *The Iron Age Camp at Poston, Vowchurch*, 1958
Cunliffe, Barry, 'The Iron Age' in *British Prehistory, a new outline*, (Ed. Colin Renfrew), 1974
Cunliffe, Barry, *Iron Age Communities in Britain* (2nd edition), 1978
Hogg, A.H.A., 'Hill Forts and Herefordshire', *TWNFC Vol. XLI(i)*, 1973
Hogg, A.H.A., *Hill Forts of Britain*, 1975
Kenyon, K.M., 'Excavations at Sutton Walls, Herefordshire 1948-51', *Archaeological Journal CX*, 1953 (includes supplementary surveys of Aconbury, Credenhill and Dinedor)
Marshall, George, 'Poston, Vowchurch: Interim Report', *TWNFC Vol. 28(i)*, 1934
Ordnance Survey, *Southern Britain in the Iron Age*, 1962
Royal Commission on Historic Monuments, *Inventories of Herefordshire, Vols. I-III*, 1931-34
(Also for Chapters VII, XII and XIII)
Stanford, S.C., 'Credenhill Camp, Herefordshire', *Archaeological Journal CXXVII*, 1970
Stanford, S.C., *Croft Ambrey*, 1974
Stanford, S.C., *Guide to Prehistoric and Roman Sites in Herefordshire*, 1976
Stanford, S.C., *The Archaeology of the Welsh Marches*, 1980
Thomas, Nicholas, *Guide to Prehistoric England*, 1960
Transactions of the Woolhope Naturalists' Field Club include notes and plans of the following sites (early dates have no volume numbers): Aconbury (1883-85); Bach Camp (1883-85); Brandon Camp (1881-82); Caplar Camp (1883-85 and 1924); Coxhall Knoll (1881-82); Croft Ambrey (1895-97 and Vols. 31-39, 1942-69); Herefordshire Beacon and Midsummer Hill (1877-80); Poston Camp (Vol. 27, 1934); Pyon Wood (1895-97); Risbury (1883-85); Wall Hills, both Bromyard and Ledbury (1883-85); and Wapley Camp (1895-97)

Chapter III
Baker, A., 'Aerial reconnaissance on the Romano-British town of Kenchester in 1956', *TWNFC Vol. 38*, 1956
Baker, A., 'Results of aerial survey in Herefordshire in 1969', *TWNFC Vol. 40*, 1970
Bird, T., 'A Roman pavement from Bishopstone in Herefordshire', *Archaeologia XXIII*, 1930
Bridgewater, N.P., 'Romano-British iron-working near Ariconium', *TWNFC Vol. 38*, 1965-66

Collingwood, R.G. and Richmond, A., *The Archaeology of Roman Britain*, 1969

Frere, S.S., *Britannia*, 1974

Heys, F.H. and Thomas, M., 'Excavations of the defences of Kenchester', *TWNFC Vols. 36 and 37*, 1958 and 1963

Jack, G.H., *Excavations on the site of Ariconium*, 1924

Jarrett, M.G. (ed.), *The Roman Frontier in Wales*, 1969

Margary, I.D., *Roman Roads in Britain*, 1967

Martin, S.H., 'Roman coins found in Herefordshire', *TWNFC Vol. 34*, 1954

Moore, H.C., 'Roman roads and the so-called Julian road'; 'Watling Street in Herefordshire', *TWNFC Vol. 19(ii)*, 1903

Ordnance Survey, *Map of Roman Britain*, 4th edition, 1978

Rivet, A.L.F., 'The British section of the Antonine Itinerary', *Britannia I*, 1970

Rivet, A.L.F., and Smith, Colin, *The Place-names of Roman Britain*, 1981

Rodwell, W., and Rowley, T. (Eds.), *The Small Towns of Roman Britain*, 1975

Stanford, S.C., 'The Roman forts at Leintwardine and Buckton', *TWNFC Vol. 39*, 1968
  see also Chapter II

Tacitus, Cornelius (Trans. Michael Grant), *The Annals of Imperial Rome*, 1983

Webster, Graham, 'The Roman Military advance under Ostorius Scapula', *Archaeological Journal CXV*, 1958

Wilmott, A.R., 'Kenchester *(Magnis)*: A Reconsideration', *TWNFC Vol. 43 (i)*, 1980

Wood, James G., 'Primary Roman Roads into Herefordshire etc.,' *TWNFC Vol. 19 (ii)*, 1903

Chapter IV

Ashley, Maurice, *The Life and Times of William I*, 1973

Bannister, A.T., *The Place-Names of Herefordshire*, 1916

Ekwall, Eilert, *The Concise Oxford Dictionary of Place-names*, 4th edition, 1980

Hillaby, Joseph, 'The Origins of the Diocese of Hereford', *TWNFC Vol. 42 (iii)*, 1978

Moore, H.C., 'Offa's Dyke and Watt's Dyke', *TWNFC Vol. 19 (iii)*, 1904

Noble, Frank, *The ODA Book of Offa's Dyke Path*, 1981

Watkins, Alfred, 'Offa's Dyke and the gap in the Weobley District', *TWNFC Vol. 19 (iii)*, 1904

Chapter V

Chibnall, M., *The Ecclesiastical History of Ordericus Vitalis*, 1973

de Gray Birch, Walter, *Vita Haroldi*, 1885

Freeman, Edward A., *History of the Norman Conquest, Vols. ii-iii*, 1867-79

Garmonsway, G.N. (Ed.), *The Anglo-Saxon Chronicle*, 1978

Giles, John A., 'Vita Haroldi', *Vita Quorundum*, 1854

Stenton, Sir Frank, *The Bayeux Tapestry*, 1965

Chapter VI

Bannister, A.T., 'The Herefordshire Domesday', *TWNFC Vol. 19 (iii)*, 1904

Darby, H.C. and Terrett, I.B., *The Domesday Geography of Midland England (II)*, 2nd edition, 1978

Gwynne, T.A., 'Domesday Society in Herefordshire', *TWNFC Vol. 41 (i)*, 1973

Morris, John (Ed.), *Domesday Book No. 17: Herefordshire* (edited by Frank and Caroline Thorn), 1983

Walker, David, 'Hereford and the Laws of Breteuil', *TWNFC Vol. 40 (i)*, 1970

Chapter VII

Bannister, A.T., 'Richard's Castle and the Normans in Herefordshire', *TWNFC Vol. 25*, 1925

Brooke, Christopher; Gem, Richard; and Zarnecki, George (et al), *English Romanesque Art 1066-1200*, Hayward Gallery, 1984

Davis, R.H.C., *The Normans and their Myth*, 1976

Davison, Brian K., 'Early earthwork castles, a new model', *Chateau Gaillard (iii)*, Ed. A.J. Taylor, 1969

Platt, Colin, *Medieval Britain from the Air*, 1984

Tonkin, J.W., 'Herefordshire Castles', *TWNFC Vol. 44 (i)*, 1982

Chapter VIII

Bingham, Caroline, *The Life and Times of Edward II*, 1973

Dictionary of National Biography (s.n.)

Holmes, George A., *The Estates of the higher nobility in the 14th century*, 1957

Hopkins, Gordon, *Wigmore and Places of Interest Nearby*, 1983

Hutchinson, John, 'Sir Roger and other Mortimers', *Herefordshire Biographies*, 1890

Owen, Henry, *The Administration of English Law in Wales and the Marches*, 1900

Planche, J.R., *The Conqueror and his Companions (2 vols.)*, 1874

Chapter IX

Midmer, Roy, *English Medieval Monasteries*, 1979

Musset, Lucien, *Abbayes et Prieurés de Normandie: Abbaye Notre-Dame de Mortemer*, 1979

Tonkin, J.W., 'The nunnery of Limebrook and its property', *TWNFC Vol. 41 (ii)*, 1974

Tonkin, J.W., 'Religious Houses with reference to Herefordshire', *TWNFC Vol. 44 (ii)*, 1983

Chapter X

Arlott, J. (Ed.), *John Speed's England*, 1953

Aston, Michael and Bond, James, *The Landscape of Towns*, 1976

Biddle, M. and Hill, D., 'Late Saxon planned towns', *Antiquaries Journal Vol. 51 (i)*, 1971

City of Hereford Archaeology Committee, *The defences of Hereford: Mill Street-St Owen's Street*, 1980

Enumerators' Returns, *National Census (Hereford) 1841-1881*, (Microfilm at County Record Office)

Hillaby, Joe, 'The Norman new town of Hereford, its street pattern and European context', *TWNFC Vol. 44 (ii)*, 1983

Jancey, E.M., *The Royal Charters of the City of Hereford*, 1973

Lobel, M.D., *Historic Towns Atlas: Hereford Vol I*, 1969

Sandford, Anne, and Shoesmith, Ron, *Hereford, Archaeology in the City*, 1975

Sandford, Anne, *Hereford As it Was*, (photographs), 1984

Spiers, David, 'The street names of Hereford 1757-1961,' *TWNFC Vol. 37 (ii)*, 1962

West, John, *Town Records*, 1983

Chapter XI

Beresford, Maurice and Finberg, H.P.R., *English Medieval Boroughs, A Handlist*, 1973

Hillaby, Joseph, 'The Boroughs of the Bishop of Hereford in the late 13th century, with particular reference to Ledbury', *TWNFC Vol. 40 (i)*, 1970

Hillaby, Joseph, 'The parliamentary borough of Weobley, 1628-1708', *TWNFC Vol.39*, 1967

Hillaby, Joseph and Pearson, Edna D., *Bromyard: A Local History*, 1970

Hillaby, Joseph and Pearson, Edna D., *The Book of Ledbury*, 1982

Price, John, *An Historical and Topographical Account of Leominster and its Vicinity*, 1975

Phillott, Henry Wright, *Notes on Weobley*, 1869

Reeves, N.C., *Leominster, the Town in the Marches*, n.d.

Salt, A.E.W., *The Borough and Honour of Weobley*, 1953

Strong, George, *Handbook to Ross and Archenfield*, 1863

Townsend, G.F., *The Town and Borough of Leominster*, 1863

Williams, W.R., *Herefordshire Members 1213-1896*, 1896

Wydean Tourist Board, *A Walk around Ross-on-Wye* (Information Sheet No. 13), 1984

Chapter XII

Royal Commission on Historical Monuments, *Inventories of Herefordshire, Vols. I-III*, 1931-34

Yarwood, Doreen, *English Costume*, 1958

also church guides *passim*

Chapter XIII

Note: The publications marked * are available on sale at the houses which they describe

Andere, Mary, *Homes and Houses of Herefordshire*, 1977

Aslet, Clive, 'Dinmore Manor, Herefordshire', *Country Life*, April 18, 1985

Croft, O.G.S., *The House of Croft of Croft Castle*, 1949

Finola, Lady Somers and Elizabeth Hervey Bathurst, *Eastnor Castle, Ledbury, Herefordshire*, n.d.*

Lees-Milne, James, *Berrington Hall*, National Trust, 1982*

Murray, Richard Hollins, *Dinmore Manor*, 1936*

Pevsner, N., *Herefordshire* in *The Buildings of England* series, 1963

Reid, Peter, *Burke and Saville's Guide to Country Houses, Vol. 2*, 1980

Robinson, Rev. Charles J., *Mansions and Manors of Herefordshire*, 1873

Uhlman, Diana, *Croft Castle*, National Trust, 1982*

Chapter XIV

Aylmer, G.E., 'Who was ruling Herefordshire from 1645 to 1661?', *TWNFC Vol. 40 (iii)*, 1972

Faraday, M.A., 'Shipmoney in Herefordshire', *TWNFC Vol.41 (ii)*, 1974

Fraser, Antonia, *Weaker Vessels*, 1984 (For Lady Brilliana Harley)

Heath-Agnew, E., *Royalist to Roundhead: A Biography of Colonel John Birch (1615-1691)*, 1977

Hutchinson, John, 'John and Barnabas Scudamore' and 'Sir Robert and Sir Edward Harley', *Herefordshire Biographies*, 1890

James, F.R., 'The Diary of Joyce Jefferies (1638-47),' *TWNFC Vol. 24*, 1922

Keeler, M.F., *The Long Parliament 1640-1641*, 1954

La Touche, Rev. J.D., 'Brampton Bryan Castle: its sieges and demolition', *TWNFC Vol.10*, 1881-82

Lewis, Thomas Taylor (Ed.), *The Letters of Brilliana Harley*, Camden Society, 1853

Latham, R., *The Diaries of Samuel Pepys*, 11 volumes to 1983

Matthews, A.G. (Ed.), *Walker Revised*, 1948 from 'An attempt towards the recovery of an account of the sufferings of the clergy ... etc.', 1714

Thomason Tracts c.1641 ff., Birmingham Reference Library microfilm 1091(4)

Webb, J. and T., *Memorials of the Civil War ... as it affected Herefordshire and the adjacent counties*, 1879

Webb, T.W., *Military Memoirs of Colonel John Birch*, Camden Society, 1873

Chapter XV

Barley, M., *The English Farmhouse and Cottage*, 1972

Morgan, F.C., 'A Hereford Bookseller's Catalogue of 1695', *TWNFC Vol. 31 (i)*, 1942

Morgan, F.C., 'A Hereford Mercer's Inventory of 1689', *TWNFC Vol. 31 (iii)*, 1944

Morgan, F.C., 'Inventories of a Hereford saddler's shop, 1692 and 1696', *TWNFC Vol. 31 (iv)*, 1945

West, John, *Village Records*, 1982

Chapter XVI

Berridge, Elizabeth (Ed.), *The Early Diary of Elizabeth Barrett Browning*, 1974

Clew, Kenneth R., *Bredwardine, Hereford: A Brief Guide*, 1980

Cobbett, William, *Rural Rides 1821-1832*, 1885

Defoe, Daniel, *Tour Through Great Britain*, 1724-26

Fiennes, Celia (Ed. Trevelyan, G.M.), *The Journeys of Celia Fiennes*, 1947

Kilvert, Francis (Ed. William Plomer), *Kilvert's Diary: (Selections from 1970-1879)*, 1938

Leland, John (Ed. Toulmin Smith, Lucy), *Itinerary in Wales (1535-1543), Vol iv*, 1907-1910

Watkins, Alfred, 'Elizabeth Barrett and Hope End', *TWNFC Vol. 25*, 1925

Chapter XVII

Gray, H.L., *English Field Systems*, 1959

Parker, W.K., 'Opposition to Parliamentary enclosure in Herefordshire, 1793-1815', *TWNFC Vol. 44 (i)*, 1982

Tate, W.E., 'A Handlist of Herefordshire Enclosure Acts and Awards', *TWNFC Vol. 30*, 1941

Watkins, Charles, 'The Parliamentary enclosure of Much Marcle', *TWNFC Vol. 43 (iii)*, 1981

Chapter XVIII

As for *Chapter XVI*. Also:

Bates, Alan, *Directory of Stage Coach Services*, 1969

David & Charles, *Reprint of the first edition of the one-inch Ordnance Survey of England and Wales, Sheet No. 50 Leominster (Ludlow, Kidderminster), 1832, Sheet No. 59 Hereford (Gloucester, Monmouth), 1831*

Hereford Times 1830-1880 (passim), Hereford City Library

Jenkins, Rhys, 'Industries of Herefordshire in Bygone Times', *TWNFC Vol. 29*, 1937

Local Acts 1730-1828, County Record Office

Ogilby, John, *Britannia*, 1675

Partridge, Edward J., *The Route of the Shrewsbury & Hereford Railway*, 1860

Paterson's Roads, 1808-1828 editions

Pigot & Co's National Commercial Directory 1830, includes Herefordshire

Chapter XIX

Baylis, Ebenezer & Sons, *A Picturesque Guide to Hereford*, 1899

Cassey, Edward, *History, Topography and Directory of Herefordshire*, 1858

Dodd, J. Philip, 'Herefordshire agriculture in the mid-nineteenth century', *TWNFC Vol. 43 (ii)*, 1980

Gaze, Janet, *Yesterday in Ewyas Harold*, 1981

Hopkinson, Jean, *Little Cowarne, A Herefordshire Village*, 1983

Lascelles & Co Ltd, *Directory of Hereford 1851*

Chapter XX

Beck, K.M., *West Midland Lines of the GWR: 2. 'Rails to Hereford'*, 1983

Bromyard & District Local History Society, *Bromyard the Day Before Yesterday: A Book of Photographs*, 1979

Census of 1861 (West Midlands): Occupations Analysis

Collins, William, *Herefordshire and the Great War*, 1919

General Register Office, *Census 1961, England and Wales: Occupation, Industry, Socio-Economic Groups: Herefordshire*, HMSO, 1966

Gurney, –, *Graphic Guide to Hereford*, 1912

Hereford Journal, The, 1900-1914 *passim*

Roberts, Graham (Ed.), *Hereford Official Guide*, 5th edition, 1980

Index

125

126